Chronicles of a Serial Dater

ANN•MARIE SORRELL

Published by

Sorrell Management Enterprise, LLC
2930 Okeechobee Blvd, Ste 207
West Palm Beach, Florida 33409

Chronicles of a Serial Dater
ISBN-13: 978-0997597608
ISBN-10: 0997597607

Printed in the United States of America.

10 9 8 7 6 5 4 3 2 1

Library of Congress Cataloging-in-Publication Data
Library of Congress Control Number [LCCN]: 201696379

First Edition February 2017

Book Cover & Layout Design by Danté D. Fillyau of MediumFour
Fort Lauderdale, Florida

This book is available at quantity discounts for bulk purchases.
For information, call 561.531.4046

www.chroniclesofaserialdater.com

DEDICATION & SPECIAL THANKS

This memoir is dedicated to my mother, my five sisters, best girlfriends, aunts and friends across the globe.

We have all been on our respective dating journeys. We have experienced the good, bad, ugly and funny of trying to meet Mr. Right. Many of you have met your Mr. Wonderful, your life partner, and I congratulate and continue to learn from you. I know it has been quite the journey, but nonetheless, you survived it! For those of us still searching or just not quite sure if we have found The One, let the force be with us!

Special thanks to my male friends, ex-boyfriends and acquaintances. Thank you for your insight, time, and experiences. This would not be possible without you!

CONTENTS

INTRODUCTION

As we go through life we cross paths with people who become our friends, lovers, admirers and life partners. We experience like, lust, infatuation and love. Some of us even experience obsession. In our dating lives, we often wonder, will he choose me? Should I choose him? Why didn't he choose me? We drive ourselves crazy with these questions.

Some of us make our decisions based on height, weight, hair, fashion sense, smile, good or bad breath, dark or light complexion, rich or broke. Some of us choose based on whether our potential mate is selfless, honest and humble.

Our choices make us laugh, cry or just thank God we didn't end up with "that person." My first boyfriend, Andrew, turned out to be a seven-year-old girl beater. Nevertheless, we date.

I've met many men. Some never made it to the first date. Others made it through several months, even a couple of years. Each experience was different and memorable.

Men who didn't get what they wanted have called me mean, picky, shallow, vain, bougie and self-centered. But a girl wants what she wants, right? Should I settle for less? I tried to give some men the benefit of the doubt and a fair chance, figuring they could turn out to be Mr. Right. But most did not.

Join me as I reflect on the twists and turns of my dating journey.

I hope you will be able to reminisce, laugh and relate to the experiences I will share in this labor of love.

To women everywhere who have taken the time to support and read my book, I pray that you enjoy it and share the lessons with others. To the fellas, please read these stories with an open mind and be ready to laugh and learn.

A special note to the guys: If something sounds familiar and you are wondering, "Is she talking about me?" More than likely I am.

A BOX OF NEWPOATS

When I hear Salt-n-Pepa's Shoop, especially the line, "You, the bow-legged one," I can't help but think of Lawrence. He was tall, slim, cute, and bow-legged. I was 14 and thought I was the best thing since sliced bread. In my mind I could have any boy I wanted, and most of the time I did. And I wanted Lawrence.

I was "thick" with long beautiful hair and smooth butter pecan skin. I also had bigger breasts than other girls my age. I can hear my elders saying, "She was just hot in the ass and fast!" It was infatuation at first sight for both of us. Things were simple then. Boy meets girl. Boy likes girl. Boy and girl become a couple. There was no pressure for sex. If the question came up, we girls would always say, "You have to wait at least six months," knowing it probably would not last that long. Lawrence and I dated on and off for about 18-months but didn't have sex. The clock started over each time we were on again. Being a playerette, most of our break-ups were my fault. Lawrence often caught me talking to other boys. I always made up some excuse, but when he caught me with the same boy again, we'd break up. He would leave and I would get another boyfriend.

Lawrence had graduated high school and was trying to figure out what to do with his life. He was in and out of town, often for months at a time. As soon as he came back, though, I would break up with whomever I was with to go back to him. He had some serious control over my emotions.

What was so special about Lawrence? He was thoughtful, had a sense of humor and got along with all my friends. He did things for me the average boy my age couldn't, such as paying my beeper bill, buying me jewelry and giving me money. I had something to brag about, especially considering I didn't have to sleep with him. Lawrence respected me enough to not want to take my innocence until I was ready. That wasn't happening anytime soon as my mom would kill me.

I will never forget the day it ended for good. There was a big celebration at the Martin Luther King, Jr. park to honor NFL legend and Hall of Famer, Rickey Jackson who'd come back to our hometown, Pahokee, Florida. I was hanging out with my friends and he was hanging out with his when a girl whom I was in the O.D. Express Marching band with told me that Lawrence was her man. I was not going to trip on her, so I called Lawrence to the side and confronted him. "Are you her man?" I asked. He acted nonchalant and started talking loudly. He pulled out a box of Newport cigarettes and said, "Baby, you like a box of Newpoats. Smoke one up and get another when I want to. So get out my face with this shit."

I was embarrassed and hurt. I told him it was over and that I would not be disrespected as I walked away trying to hold my head high. Lawrence later tried to apologize but it was too late. I realized my feelings were not as strong as they had been. Although he bought me things and had been kind and respectful, we were not on the same page. I still had a couple years of high school and needed to plan for college. I also realized I was feeling the same pain I'd inflicted on the guys I'd done wrong each time Lawrence came back into my life. He was not the person for me anymore and I was over him.

Tips for the Ladies: Sometimes, your ego must take a hit for you to get clarity and realize a relationship isn't for you. When there is no growth and both parties are at a fork in the road, it's time to move on. Also, don't confront your man in public. You might get embarrassed.

Tips for the Fellas: Don't embarrass your girlfriend in public. You might lose her for good. Also, when you realize the two of you are no longer compatible, move on before seeing someone new.

FRIENDLY COMPETITION

He was dark, handsome, and athletic. We called him All-Star Wayne. All the girls in my sophomore class wanted him. He had graduated high school a couple years earlier and was a great basketball player who hadn't gone to college. Five of us had a competition to see who would get him first. Whenever we would see Wayne, everyone but me would speak. He would smile and keep on riding.

My strategy was to turn my head the other way and look disinterested. One day, three of us were walking on our block when we saw him. My two best friends went out of their way to speak to Wayne as I strolled behind, again paying him no attention. I could see him glancing at me. The street lights were on and it was past my curfew so I told everyone goodnight. The next day, my friend was excited as she told me how he walked her home. She thought Wayne liked her. I was cool, figuring she won the competition.

The next evening, Wayne walked down our block again. He slowly eased into a conversation with me. Next thing I knew, he was asking to walk me home. He said that he had his eyes on me all along. I didn't know how to respond. I liked him but so did my friend. I didn't want to hurt her. I asked him about his interest in her. He told me he was interested in me and I should give him a chance. Wayne leaned in and gave me a kiss good night. My heart melted but a part of me felt bad because I'd have to tell my friend what happened. I told her the next day. She was hurt but accepted his decision.

Wayne and I hung out for months. He taught me about football and my favorite team became the San Francisco 49ers. I met his mom and he met mine. Wayne was afraid of my mom, though. He thought she was mean. It didn't help that she embarrassed the hell out of him the first time he came to our house. My mom had a rule that everyone must take off their shoes when they entered. Wayne followed the rule. My mom came into the living room and said in patois, "A wah smell suh? A yuh foot smell suh?" (What smells like that? Is it your feet that smells like that?) She grabbed a can of air freshener and began spraying it everywhere. Wayne was so embarrassed he put on his shoes and left immediately. From that day on, my mom called him "tink foot Wayne" (Stink feet Wayne).

We survived the embarrassment and Wayne turned out to be nice and respectful. He was totally in love. There was nothing he wouldn't do for me. It could be raining, hot as hell or freezing cold and he would ride his bike or walk to see me every day. I was really feeling him, too, and thought I was in love. Time seemed to stop when we were together. When we kissed it seemed to last for hours. One day, we were watching Married with Children and kissed through two episodes nonstop. Wayne had the best kisses ever! He was patient and did not pressure me to have sex. What a great guy.

One evening, as Wayne walked me home, I saw in the distance the silhouette of a tall, slim, bow-legged figure. My heart began beating fast as we drew closer and crossed paths with Lawrence. Lawrence greeted us and kept walking. Wayne knew my history with Lawrence. He looked at me and asked whether I knew he was back in town. I said, "No," and assured him I didn't care if he was. I only wanted him.

Within days, Lawrence called and told me to cut Wayne off. I felt horrible even considering his demand. He was asking me to choose with no regard for my feelings for Wayne or his for me. It was a hard decision considering the strong feelings I had for Wayne. However, I did exactly what Lawrence told me to and dumped him.

As Wayne walked me home one evening, I gave him the cold shoulder. I pretended not to want him to touch or talk to me. When he asked why I was acting that way I said I didn't like him anymore and we should just be friends. He stopped and stared into my eyes. "But I thought you said you loved me," he said. "I love you."

"I never loved you," I replied, coldly. "It was all a lie."
He asked if Lawrence was the reason my feelings had changed. I lied again.
"No, I just do not want you anymore. It was all a part of a bet and I won."
I had never seen a man cry. Tears started streaming down Wayne's face as he begged me not to treat him that way.

Deep down, I was hurt, too. I didn't mean a word. That was Lawrence speaking, not me.

I knew Wayne was a good guy who really cared about me. He didn't pay attention to other girls. He made it clear to everyone I was the only girl for him.
But I was still stuck on Lawrence. You know how that ended.
After I broke up with Lawrence, I begged Wayne to take me back. Yes, I begged.

At first, he would only talk to me for a few minutes but I didn't give up. I called Wayne every day. It took almost six months of asking him to take me back before he eventually gave in and gave me a second chance. Getting back with Wayne, though, came with the drama of girls wanting to fight me over him, so I changed my mind again. Bad, I know. Although he tried to assure me that it was me he wanted, I was not going to get into fist fights with those chicks over him.

I deserved for Wayne not to want me back. I took him for granted and he had done nothing wrong. He eventually forgave me, and after more than 14 years, whenever our paths cross, I still manage to make him blush.

Tips for the Ladies: As cliché as it sounds, the grass is not always greener on the other side. Sometimes we are too young or dumb or both to realize when we have a good thing right there in front of us. So we take people for granted. We think they will always be there as a fall back. Even if they are there, the relationship will never be the same. When you have the opportunity to choose, weigh the pros and cons and choose wisely. You may never get a second chance.

Tips for the Fellas: Wayne did everything right. Some may say he was weak but I believe he was genuine and expressed his true feelings. If you give your heart and still lose the girl, remember it's her loss. Wayne wasn't the loser here. I was.

DON'T JUMP IN THE OCEAN IF YOU CAN'T SWIM

I was working part time at a grocery store my senior year when I met John, a would-be rapist.

I was in the band, senior class president and involved in numerous extracurricular activities on campus. Life was good.

Until John gave me the worst scare of my 17 years.

He was in his late twenties or early thirties. I was an early bloomer and mentally mature, so I always attracted older men. John was cute. He flirted with me in the check-out line.
For two weeks, he would come by the store every night. I knew I had no business talking to him, but I gave him my number anyway. It's not like I planned to have sex with him. Besides, I'd be leaving soon for college.

We talked often. He would pick me up from work, take me home after football games, give me money for school trips and events and visit me at home when my mom was at work. This went on for a few months. John and I would play around and kiss, but that was the limit. I told him I was a virgin even though I'd had sex once a couple years before.

On Christmas Eve, John picked me up to grab a bite and see the Christmas lights. We ate our Taco Bell at a park. John noticed I was wearing red tights under my jean skirt "You know red is my favorite color," he said. "I have waited long enough, you are coming out of those tights tonight." I smiled and responded in my most innocent voice. "No, I'm not." John insisted he was going to be my first. I tried to avoid it by pointing out he didn't have condoms. "Of course not," he said. "I have a wife. Why would I ride around with condoms." "A wife!" I yelled. "You never told me you were married!"

"You didn't need to know, he said. She was always out of town. It doesn't matter, you are still coming out of your tights." I was getting more nervous by the minute.

I asked him to take me home. He started the car, drove a few blocks and stopped at a gas station. They didn't have what he needed. He drove to another gas station. They had it. He pulled out three condoms.

I was scared as hell. I began to plead with John to take me home. He started driving a different route from the one we'd taken. He turned into a park just below Lake Okeechobee. It was dark and isolated. When I asked him why we were there John said he had to pee. I thought about jumping from his truck and running but where? It was dark. Cell phones weren't ubiquitous then. I didn't know what to do.

John returned and began driving up a hill. As we approached the top, all I could see was the dark water of Lake Okeechobee. He drove slowly down the hill. "Don't jump in the ocean," he said, "if you can't swim." My heart was racing and my palms sweating as tears flowed from my eyes. John drove to the edge. "You are going to come out of those tights," he said, or swim, tonight." I begged. "John, please do not do this. I am so sorry. I did not mean to lead you on. I am not ready for this. Please take me home."

He repeatedly told me, "No." He moved closer. "I told you not to jump in the ocean if you can't swim." The tears kept coming. I pulled away from him. John opened his glove compartment and showed me a gun. "I am telling you again," he said, "either I get what I want or you swim." I sat in silence for what seemed like an eternity. Finally, I asked John again to please take me home. He stared into my eyes as if he was searching my soul. He closed the glove compartment, put the truck in reverse and told me I better not do that to him again.

John drove me home in silence. Once in front of my house, he grabbed by face, forced me to kiss him then told me to get out. I slammed the door and said, "Fuck you!"
I didn't tell my mom. She would have called the police and I was scared of what he might come back and do to me. I never spoke to John again. He called me and left several apology messages. He went by my job and my house several times and just sat in the parking lot. He finally gave up when I told him I was going to call the police if he showed up again.

I went to college that fall. When I returned for the holiday break, I ran into a friend who had worked with John. John had told him what he did to me. He was glad John hadn't raped me. He shared with me that John was in jail for raping a young lady at gunpoint at the same park he had threatened me. And rumor had it John had HIV.
I was speechless and numb. I realized how much danger I'd been in. I could have lost my life that night. God's grace saved me. I felt bad for the woman he raped. Prosecutors eventually dropped the charges, claiming it was "consensual sex."

Tips for the Ladies: Always report attacks and attempted attacks of every kind, especially rape. You could keep someone else from becoming a victim.

Tips for the Fellas: It is just wrong to prey on young girls and to force a woman of any age into sex. "She led me on" is no excuse. No means no. If you have a problem with that word seek help. A man who forces himself on a woman isn't looking for sex; he's looking for power and has mental health issues.

HAVE YOUR CAKE AND EAT IT TOO

It was sophomore year in college at Florida A&M University and of all places to get a job, I worked at a pawn shop. It was an interesting gig. I met many people, especially students, who were always pawning personal items for quick cash loans. There were also many loyal shoppers that came in on a weekly basis to get new bargains. After being there for about eight months, I met Jesse. Jesse was not very tall, 5'9, slim but cute. Not double take cute, average guy cute. He stopped in to look around and we ended up flirting. He returned the next day to get my number. I was digging his personality so I gave him the digits.

Jesse and I began to hang out a few times a week. Early on he told me things that didn't add up, such as he was a student at Florida State University. When I asked about his classes, he claimed he was taking the semester off, but doing part-time maintenance work on the campus. When I asked about going to his apartment, he said, "My boys sell drugs - but I don't - and they don't want females coming to the house because they don't want to be set up." The red light was flashing but I told myself, "Whatever. We're cool. It's not like I'm trying to marry the guy."

Jesse soon got the boyfriend title. He earned it taking my roommate and me out to dinner several times a week, buying us groceries and coming over to cook. He made the best steak and potatoes. I can't forget his fruit salad. When you're a college student, this is living large. Much better than eating Ramen Noodles every night. Every few weeks, he'd give me a couple hundred dollars to buy myself "something nice." He spent several nights a week at my apartment. Sounds like a great guy, right?

One morning around 6:15, my home phone rang. "May I speak to Jesse?" said the female voice on the other end. Surprised but calm, I rolled over and handed the phone to Jesse. "Hello," he said. "What? I'm not talking about this right now. Bye." He handed me the phone to hang up. It rang again. "May I speak to Jesse?"

I looked at the caller ID as I handed Jesse the phone. It read Chick Fil-A.
"I don't want to talk to you right now," he said, and again handed me the phone. No sooner than I hung up, it rang a third time.

"Honey," I said calmly, "Jesse is on my time right now so please talk to him on yours."
"He is my baby daddy," she said, "and we have been together since 1998." It was 2000.
"Once again," I said, this time my voice tinged with surprise and anger, "speak with Jesse on your time, and please do not call my house again."

I turned to Jesse and shot him daggers. "Who is that and how did she get my number?"
"I used to talk to her, but I don't anymore," he said calmly, "and I am not sure how she got your number. She must have gotten it from one of my boys."
I repeated what she told me. Jesse denied it, saying he only had the one son in Orlando he'd already told me about. I suggested we go to Chick-Fil-A as we were not going back to sleep until we resolved the matter.

We got up and went to Chick Fil-A. The young lady reportedly went home sick right before we arrived. Jesse then assured me that he would handle it. Although, I said OK, I kept it in the back of my mind.

My birthday and Valentine's Day were coming up and I didn't want any drama to spoil those important days. I didn't trip or investigate further at that time.

For my birthday – February 7th – Jesse gave me two-hundred dollars to buy an outfit and took me to dinner and a movie. We had hot steamy sex in the new red lingerie I bought with the money. On Valentine's Day, I came home to a trail of rose petals that led to my bedroom, a red velvet cake, red roses and balloons on my bed. When I responded to a knock on my door, Jesse was there with a box of chocolates. He had coordinated with my roommate Latisha. How thoughtful.

As I prepared to take a shower, Jesse went under my mattress, pretending to look for something he lost. He pulled out a jewelry box. I smiled wide and excitedly opened the box to find a beautiful gold bracelet. Jesse fastened it around my wrist. We went to dinner and had a fabulous evening.

About a week later, Jesse asked me to take him to the train station. He was going to see his son in Orlando. After class, on my way to pick up Jesse, I stopped at my favorite place for lunch, Chick Fil-A. I saw a young lady and wondered if she was Toya, the mystery caller and alleged baby mama. After placing my order, I asked if her name was Toya.
 "Yes" she said. "Are you Amarie?"

Toya revealed that she had gotten my number from Jesse's wallet after he started spending nights away from home. They lived together and had been a couple for two years. She was four months pregnant with his child. She had found movie ticket stubs in his pockets, dinner receipts, and receipts for things he hadn't given her.

She apologized for calling my home. She was sick and needed him. On Valentine's Day morning, Jesse dropped off a cake, balloons and items from Victoria Secret. She didn't see him again until the next day. Toya was almost in tears.

What an asshole! How could he be so insensitive and cruel to the woman carrying his child? I told her I was on my way to pick him up and would bring him by to set the record straight. I was done with him.

I picked up Jesse and smiled as if nothing had happened. "Damn, I forget my ice cream," I shouted as we approached Chick-Fil-A. "I gotta stop and get it." Jesse urged me to keep going as he was going to be late. I insisted on stopping.
It dawned on Jesse what I was doing. He became uneasy. "Oh, I see what you are up to," he said, "but I don't have shit to say to either of you."
I laughed as I approached the drive thru window.

Toya: "Hello, Jesse."
Me: "Oh, you two know each other?"
Toya: "Did you get my check off the dresser?"
Me: "The dresser? Not the one that you both share?"
Toya: "Amarie don't take him to the bank because he will try to cash my check."
Me: "I will not be taking him anywhere because he is getting his trifling ass out of my car right now!"
Jesse: "I am not getting out of your car and you are taking me to the bus station."
Me: "I am not taking you anywhere. You can walk for all I care. If you do not get out, the police will get you out."

I dialed 9-1, giving him a chance to get out before pressing the second 1.

Jesse began to apologize, begging me not to leave him. He wanted me and only me.

I was not trying to hear it. He finally got out of my car after a long, awkward moment of silence. He called for several weeks, leaving messages, asking for forgiveness and to be a part of my life. I could never bring myself to speak with him again. My conscience would not allow it. All I could think was that young, hurting pregnant woman could've been me.

Tips for the Ladies: If a man has a girlfriend, especially one he lives with and treats like shit to be with you, leave him alone. Ditto, if he has a wife. What he does to one woman he will do to you. Karma is a bitch, and you don't want that kind of negative energy.
Jesse showed signs that he wasn't honest. I ignored them because he was taking care of my needs. Pay attention to the flashing red lights. They are stop signs!

Tips for the Fellas: You cannot have your cake and eat it, too. How long do you think it will last before the truth comes out? My mother always said, "Whatever is done in the dark shall come to light." Tell women the truth upfront and let them decide if we they want to be involved with you. Don't take away their right to choose. Treat women the way you would want a man to treat your mother, sister, or daughter.

NICE GUYS FINISH LAST

Computer love began for me sophomore year with CollegeClub. com. It was great to go online and chat with Florida A&M students and those from other colleges. You could be sitting right next to someone, chatting with them and not know.

One day, I received an instant message from a username I had not seen before, tcam1980. He was cute. According to his profile, he attended my school and was a biology/ pre-med major. "He must be smart," I thought. We began to chat and over the next few days emailed each other until he asked if we could meet.

Tcam1980 greeted me with the whitest teeth and a broad, pleasant smile that melted my heart. He was tall, thick, dark, and handsome - all the way from Cameroon, Africa. Mmm, Mmm, Mmm.
His real name was Thomas. He was smart, articulate and didn't have much of an accent. The first time we met, we talked for hours until three in the morning. It seemed as if we were old friends. When I asked him to leave my apartment so I could go to bed, Thomas looked at me with his big brown eyes and shocked me by softly saying, "Ann, I am in love with you."
"I don't know how y'all do it in Africa," I said, "but in America, we get to know someone first before we tell them we love them."
"In my country," he replied, "when we meet our princess and believe that she is the one, we make her our queen and I believe you are the one."

I was flattered, but not enough to believe him. "What does he want," I thought, "because I am not giving it up." We sat in silence for a few minutes before I asked him to leave again. Before going out the door, he planted the softest, most sensual kiss on my lips. Butterflies danced in my stomach. He left me with my lips out and eyes closed. In a daze, I slowly waved goodbye.

My best friend Latisha, who was also my roommate, met Thomas that night and liked him. I told her what happened and she suggested that I give him a chance. She had good instincts and felt he was a good person.

We dated for about five months. Thomas was respectful and patient. I was practicing Christianity and was trying to "live right," so I told him we couldn't have sex. He understood and respected my decision. He did not always make it easy but he didn't pressure me. Although we didn't have intercourse, Thomas wanted me to teach him how to give oral sex. I was no expert, but had some experience so I figured I could coach him. He was a good student and enjoyed learning to please me. He took pride in the fact that I was the first girl he had done that to, especially since he was so in love with me.

Thomas was very helpful and assisted me with studying, running errands for my family and chores around my apartment. He did not want me to lift a pin. I found it annoying and repeatedly told him I did not need him. Once, he asked three times to help me hang a picture. It aggravated me so much I yelled, "I got it, now go sit down somewhere!"

My roommate looked at me and shook her head in disbelief. But I didn't care. Thomas did not yell back or get upset. He just sat down patiently. At that point, I knew I could do whatever I wanted and he would still be there.

Mr. Wonderful had arrived. He was there for me when I was sick with the flu. He was understanding about my limited time and helped me study when I was pledging my sorority, Kappa Psi Psi, so I wouldn't fall behind on my work. Thomas hung out with my family and friends at football games and other outings. They all loved him. He was too good to be true.

He began talking about us getting married and having children after graduation. The thought scared the shit out of me! I was not trying to settle down. Surely, I would have other guys who were as good to me as Thomas to choose from when I was ready. Right?
I broke up with Thomas and told him we could only be friends.

So what was wrong with Thomas? Looking back, NOTHING, ABSOLUTELY NOTHING! I made excuses. He was too nice. Too good to be true. Something had to be wrong with him. Maybe, he eats cats and monkeys in Africa. (Yes, I was silly like that). I had to teach him everything. He called too much. I wasn't ready to be married and so on.

The truth is I was young, naïve and afraid of commitment. Moreover, I didn't believe I deserved the best because I didn't know what the best looked like. I couldn't recognize what I had in front of me. I was a 20-year-old college student always looking for what I didn't have. I didn't appreciate what I already had.

Growing up without my father, I didn't know how a man was supposed to treat me. All I knew was what my mom told me. Don't let a man beat or take advantage of me. Get my education so I could take care of myself. Have my own things, and never depend on a man. It wasn't her fault. It was all she knew.

Thomas tried very hard to convince me to keep dating him, but my mind was made up. He tried to get my family and friends to talk me into taking him back, but I was not trying to hear anything they had to say. Thomas was hurt and eventually gave up. I saw him a couple of times around campus but once I graduated, I never saw him again. Thomas has crossed my mind many times over the years. I wonder if he ever found true love and happiness. I pray I did not scar him for life and that he has forgiven me.

Tips for the Ladies: Don't be afraid of a good man and don't take him for granted. You deserve someone that is "too nice." You deserve to be loved wholeheartedly. Don't sell yourself short. You may never get another chance at Mr. Nice Guy.

Tips for the Fellas: If you are a nice guy, don't change. Don't let a woman who doesn't appreciate you make you bitter. Don't settle and don't be discouraged. The woman who will love and appreciate you just as you are is out there.

CAN'T SUCK A NIGGA DICK

House parties are the best social gatherings. You get a chance to hang out with old friends and meet new ones in a casual and laid back environment. House parties gave me the chance to really get to know people and form new relationships.

I met Ronnie at a house party before he became a part of my inner circle of friends. We went out together and attended each other's parties. After a party at Ronnie's house one night, he and I got into a deep discussion about politics. It was nearly two in the morning when I noticed that everyone else had gone. Ronnie insisted I stay because it was so late and I'd had several drinks. He offered to sleep on the couch and give me his bed. I was cool with that.

As I got comfortable and dozed off, I felt someone next to me. I opened my eyes and saw Ronnie. He said the couch was uncomfortable and promised to leave me alone. I asked him to stay on his side of the bed. I dozed off but a feeling of warmth at my back and hardness against my butt woke me. I asked Ronnie what he thought he was doing.

Of course, he wanted to have sex.
I told Ronnie I wasn't in the mood and wasn't attracted to him. He asked if I would give him head. I told him I didn't do that. I just wanted to go to sleep.
Five minutes later, Ronnie grabbed my hand and tried to put it on his dick. I pulled my hand away and asked him to stop. He rose above me as if he wanted to put his dick in my face. I tried to move from under him.
"You act like you can't suck a nigga dick!" he shouted.
"WOW" was all I could say. I grabbed my things and stormed out.

I never spoke to Ronnie again.

Tips for the Ladies: Take the couch, it is more than likely room for one and he will be less likely to climb on there with you unless you invite him to do so. A man's bed is an open invitation regardless of what he tells you. Better yet, call a cab and get your car later.

Tips for the Fellas: If a girl tells you NO, that is exactly what she means. Don't try to force yourself on her, especially if she tells you she is not feeling you like that. Be respectful. If a woman wants you, she will find a way to let you know. You won't have to guess.

DOSE OF YOUR OWN MEDICINE

Moving back to South Florida from Tallahassee put me in touch with my Jamaican roots. I spent a lot of time with my family, ate at the many Jamaican restaurants, went to parties and festivals and reunited with a high school friend Sonya who became my roommate. Sonya is as Jamaican as they come, from her cooking to her dates. I had never gone to Jamaican parties and clubs until I started hanging out with my friend. I had never dated Jamaican guys.

I was sipping on a Long Island iced tea at a new Jamaican spot when a tall, bald, light-skinned man with a medium build walked in. He was dressed in Palm Beach chic. I walked over to Sonya and pointed him out. "Now, he is fine. I will get to know him before we go."

I took the extended route back to my spot against the wall, giving him a slight smile as I passed by. I was rocking side to side when I noticed him looking in my direction. I locked eyes with him. He walked over with that old school bowleggedness. "Good evening," he said with a smile.

Keith was 33. He'd moved to West Palm Beach a month before from New York. We made a movie date for the next evening.

Our first date was great. Keith seemed like a cool guy. We began to spend a lot of time together. As I learned more about Keith, I found out he did not have a job. That was understandable since he'd just moved to town. He also didn't have a car. He lived with his sister and borrowed her car. No problem. He had just moved here to get a fresh start. Right?

I was in graduate school at Nova Southeastern University and working for a non-profit organization. Keith was interested in law enforcement, but had only worked as a security guard and did not have a college degree. I offered to help him. I pulled together a resume and called my uncle, who worked for the sheriff's office to see if they were hiring. They were. I told Keith to pick up an application. He asked me to. I did, but he never completed it.

Four months in, I noticed Keith was sleeping over more often and would still be at my place when I returned from work. He started borrowing my car to supposedly look for a job. Of course, I had to keep gas in the car.

I don't mind helping a brother out, especially if he's my man. But was he my man? Keith and I had fun together, great conversation and really great sex. When we met, I had not been sexually active for some time and was still a bit naïve and reserved. He taught me a lot about sex, including how to please him. He had a weird fetish. Watching me pee turned him on. Whether I was taking a piss in the toilet or in the shower, he got a kick watching me stoop and handle my business. I didn't care. Whatever floated his boat.

Five months in, I asked Keith what we were doing. He responded that he didn't want a girlfriend. He was just chilling.
Was he serious?

I told Keith that once he had sex with me, drove my car, spent the night at my house and met my family he was my man. He was not going to keep getting girlfriend benefits unless we were in a relationship. He didn't take me seriously until I cut him off. I stopped picking him up, returning his calls, and helping him with his "job search." Amarie was not having it. I didn't see Keith again until two years later.

We met for dinner and updated each other on our lives. Over the next several months, we hung out frequently. Nothing physical, just building a friendship. I learned that Keith had never loved a woman not even his first daughter's mom. He dated her for a while and then moved in with her when she got pregnant. She had a good career and took care of him. She bought his clothes, his car and whatever else he needed. She made him get a job after his daughter was born. He didn't keep one long, though, because he preferred to pursue his dream of being a music producer and DJ.

It all began to make sense. He ran the "I want to pursue my music career" game on me, too. I even sent him information from several schools including Full Sail University where I contacted the school and had a brochure mailed to my house. Keith did nothing with the brochure and application. When he told me he had invented children's toys, specifically a board game called Ludo that he wanted to sell, I set up a meeting with a friend who invents toys and sells them to Mattel, Hasbro and other toy companies. Keith didn't follow through on any of the advice. I later learned that the Board game Ludo already existed and is a popular tradition in the West Indies, especially Jamaica. Keith was not inventing anything new.

Like me, his daughter's mom got fed up and kicked him out. He had been with her for almost ten years but never loved her. What kind of bullshit is that? He said it was convenient.

Keith had recently had a child with another woman he didn't love. She was a fling. The pregnancy was unplanned. She wouldn't let him see the baby unless he agreed to be with her so he chose not to be active in his child's life.

I visited Keith one evening. He had a posh apartment. I complimented him and told him I was glad he was doing well. He was working as a security guard and had gotten a car. Then he told me about his latest affair. He was dating a nurse with five children. She had furnished his apartment and paid his cable bill each month. He was using her and wasn't interested in a serious relationship. How could he take money from a woman with five children? He said he'd been honest with her yet she still wanted to provide for him.

One evening Keith and I were talking on the phone when he told me he'd been enjoying our conversations and his feelings for me had grown. He felt that he was falling in love with me. He had never felt that way. The feeling wasn't mutual. I just wanted to be his friend. Knowing what I knew, I couldn't get involved with him again. No way could I overlook his relationship history, including the one he and I had shared years earlier.

A few weeks later, Keith got into an altercation involving the woman he was seeing. He had gone to visit her and a man was there in his pajamas. He had seen the man before but the woman said he was her son's friend. He thought the guy was too old to be her son's friend but he let it go. Turned out, the nurse was seeing and lying to them both. She chose the other guy and told Keith to leave.

Keith was sad but all I could do was laugh. I offered him a hug. He said he was OK. He didn't care about her anyway. I told him that he thought he was playing her, but all along she was playing him. About a month later, Keith moved in with his parents. Clearly, the nurse was taking care of more than his cable bill.

We lost touch. But I hope Keith learned that players get played. Eventually, everyone gets a dose of their own medicine.

Tips for the Ladies: The past matters. It's important to know a man's relationship and work history if you want a relationship with him. Knowing relationship patterns will help you stay clear of men with commitment issues. If a man has children, pay attention to how much time he spends with them. A man who doesn't take care of his children is not boyfriend or husband material. Neither is a man who can't keep a job or is always asking for help. These are sure signs that you will end up taking care of him and all of his baggage.

Tips for the Fellas: Sugar mamas are only going to take care of you for so long before they tire of your trifling ways. A real man doesn't depend on a woman – or his parents - to pay his bills. You may think you are getting over, but the person you hurt the most is yourself. In the end you will wind up alone with nothing but a list of conquests. What goes around comes around.

GONE IN 60 SECONDS

My girls and I had limited options for nightlife, so we went to the same spots regularly. We saw the same guy cliques all the time. The GQ clique. The Macho clique. The I'm-So-Important-I-Know-Everyone clique. Morris, a smooth chocolate - but not so tall - handsome brother with a knockout smile was in the I'm-So-Important clique. That was my type.

Morris was cocky as hell, cool and confident. We had met on several occasions but just had small talk. One night, he asked if we could get together. We exchanged numbers and talked for about a week. During a late night conversation, Morris invited me to his place. I hesitated. At that hour a visit meant one thing. I was a "good girl." I needed to be "in a relationship" to give it up. A close friend, Tina who was older and a little more experienced, suggested I loosen up and have fun.
What the hell, I thought. I'll just wrap it up.

Morris had a nice bachelor pad. He offered me a glass of wine and invited me upstairs. I was nervous, but curious. He whispered the things he was going to do to me. His warm breath against my neck made me tingle. He ran his fingers through my hair and slowly removed my clothes, promising to kiss me all over, do it to me all night and make me feel like I've never felt.
My seductive smile signaled my delight with his plan.
My clothes were off in seconds. Morris kissed me once on the lips and then moved to a breast as he put on a condom. Suddenly, he was inside me.
What the hell happened to kissing me all over? Was that supposed to be foreplay?
Before I could get a rhythm it was over.

What the Fuck just happened! Are you serious!

"Did you just cum?" I asked.

"Yeah, but I was so excited," he said. "Give me a minute and we will do it again. Trust me. You won't be able to handle me."

I lie on his bed in disbelief. Still, I was hopeful.

Round two did come.

Kiss, condom and in it went. Before I could even moan, it was over.

"Girl, your pussy is so tight and good," he said, "I can't control myself."

I was not flattered.

A week later, Morris invited me over again. Maybe the second time could be the charm? No. He was gone in seconds again. That was it for me. Morris was a sixty-second man who talked shit to hide the fact he wasn't good in bed.

I declined his future invitations. He stopped speaking to me, acting as if I had done him wrong. Really dude? Get your dick game up.

Tips for the Ladies: Don't let cockiness fool you. Men who brag about their sexual prowess are usually bad lovers. Those who are good in bed let their actions speak for them. Don't be scared to tell a man how to please you. If you don't he won't know and you will always be dissatisfied. A man who can't handle the truth isn't worth your cookies.

Tips for the Fellas: Don't brag, just put it down and let her brag about you. If you know you have a problem, talk to a doctor or a sex therapist who can help you learn how to sustain an erection.

FUNKY SONNY

Who would have thought I'd meet a potential date through a telemarketing sales call? That's how I met Sonny. He was offering to extend a warranty on an electronic device I had purchased. He liked my voice and how politely I'd turned him down. He lived in Gainesville, Florida and had a brother from Pahokee. I knew his brother from high school. Sonny asked if he could call me offline. I said, "yes."

Sonny and I talked on the phone for several weeks before he planned a visit to West Palm Beach. Our conversations were intriguing and stimulating. We had a lot in common.

I'd seen a few pictures of Sonny. He looked to be about 5'10," average build and average looking. The man who came to my door was about 5'8," overweight, underdressed and in need of a haircut. He clearly wasn't big on first impressions.

I invited him in and took a seat next to him on the sofa. The scent of mothballs, sweat and dirty laundry assaulted my nostrils. Fortunately, I had leather furniture.

Sonny's breath had that I-haven't eaten-all-day smell so I offered him a cold beverage. He accepted. We talked for a few moments before I offered him a stick of gum. "Are you trying to tell me something?" he asked with a smile. I wanted to say, "Can you spell halitosis?" but I smiled and said, "Of course not."

We chatted for a couple of hours. Each time he tried to move in closer, I moved away. "Are you trying to run from me?" he asked with a devilish grin. My ringing cell phone saved me. My roommate needed a favor. After she hung up, I pretended she was still on the phone and I had to take care of an emergency.

I apologized and suggested that Sonny visit with his family in the area. I'd call him when I returned. I felt terrible but couldn't take another minute of his bad hygiene. I didn't answer his calls for the rest of the weekend. Once he returned to Gainesville, I told him I had decided to pursue a relationship with someone else.

Tips for the Ladies: The first date with someone you meet online or over the phone should be in a public place for lunch, coffee or something else designed to be short. If he turns out not to look – or smell – as you imagined or you just don't vibe, you can make a quick exit.

Tips for the Fellas: Hygiene matters and first impressions are critical! Please prepare for a first date by getting a haircut, shaving, wearing fresh, clean clothes, brushing your teeth and packing breath mints. This is essential if you want a conversation that lasts longer than hello, a shot at a second date, and, of course, sex. Poor hygiene, bad breath and a sorry appearance gets you kicked to the curb with the quickness.

INSECURITY ISN'T SEXY

Douglas fell in love at first sight. He had seen me in his dream. He would not accept no for an answer. But Reggie was in his way.

My girl Tina and I were grooving to live reggae music, enjoying a beautiful vibe and flirting the night away when Reggie asked me to dance. He was tall, brown skinned, built like a running back and fine. We had met at the same club a year earlier, but never connected. I was sure we would this time.

We danced for a while and I gave Reggie my number before taking a break.

Standing by the bar, a tall, dark, handsome young man offered to buy me a drink. We talked briefly then he asked me to dance. I thought about losing the opportunity to connect with Reggie, but I didn't mind him seeing me as a challenge.

Douglas and I danced to a few songs and chatted in between. We had some chemistry. As we continued to dance and talk, Reggie approached and started talking to Douglas.

"Oh, hell no! Are they friends? I'd given them both my number. Did they roll together? Damn!"

I excused myself and went to chill with Tina. When the evening ended, Douglas insisted on walking me to my car. I told him there was no need, but he was persistent. Once we got to my car, he told me he had seen a woman who looked just like me in a dream the night before. His grandfather appeared in the dream and told him she was the one. His grandfather had passed away two weeks prior. "Yeah right," I said.

Douglas was adamant, though, and seemed genuine. We parted with a hug and goodnight. I was attracted to Douglas, but I couldn't stop thinking about Reggie.

For the next three days, Douglas called to say he was thinking about me and wanted to get to know me better. Each time, I told him that I liked Reggie and would feel bad kicking it with him while thinking about his boy. That didn't stop Douglas. He was persistent as hell.

Turns out Reggie had a girlfriend. He insisted that Douglas was a great guy and that he was really feeling me, so I decided to hear him out.

Douglas invited me out on a date but didn't have a car and lived about 45 minutes away. Nevertheless, he said he would find a way to take me out. He asked Reggie to drive him.

We ate at one of my favorite restaurants, saw a movie and played pool. Afterwards, we talked for a few hours before Reggie picked him up. We had an awesome time. I started feeling him, too.

After that first date, we talked every day and hung out every weekend for about two months. Douglas was only 19. I was 23 and had always dated older guys. He was also in the U.S. illegally from Jamaica. He had recently married a young lady to become a legal resident. She lived in a nearby city and was giving him hell because he wouldn't sleep with her or get involved in a real relationship. He delivered furniture for a living and wanted to go college.

Douglas was a caring and loving soul. Before long, he had fallen in love. He was very generous and would have given me his last. He was attentive and talked about me becoming his wife and the mother of his children. I wasn't at all ready for that. But after five months, I had fallen under his spell.

I was earning an MBA, working full time and volunteering for several organizations. I was busy during the week and some weekends. Seven months into our relationship, Douglas' behavior began to change. He started asking questions like, "Where have you been today," and "Who did you meet today?" At first, I didn't think anything of it. But it became constant. And he'd get upset when I'd go out with my friends. "Who are you going to see, Jeffrey?" he'd ask. Who the hell was Jeffrey? I didn't know, but he swore I did.

He would become withdrawn and silent at the end of what seemed like great weekends together when it was time for him to leave. "You deserve better than me," he'd say. "You are going to graduate and get with some big time businessman and forget about me." Over and over, week after week, I tried to reassure him that I wanted him and we'd work through the obstacles like his marriage and immigration status.

I never gave Douglas a reason to think I was cheating or would cheat. So I could not for the life of me understand why he would behave that way. After about two months of his inquisitions and insecurities, I began to rethink our relationship.

At the National Black MBA Conference that year in Philadelphia, I met Ralph at an after party. He was an MBA student from Atlanta. We grabbed a Philly cheesesteak after the party and talked until five in the morning. I asked his advice about Douglas. He said Douglas wasn't going to change until he achieved success and became more secure and confident. It made sense. Ralph and I decided to stay in touch.

I gave Douglas another chance when I got home. Nothing had changed.

What did I do in Philly? Who did I meet? Not what did I learn or what connections did I make. When he started with the You-deserve-better-than-me talk again, I'd had enough. Maybe he was right. Maybe I did deserve better and should get a "big time businessman."

I decided to meet his expectations and broke up with him. I handled it horribly, in the meanest, most heartless way on his birthday weekend. We went to dinner and saw a play in Miami. We had a blast. The next day, we slept late and I made him breakfast. We cuddled all day then I made him a candlelight dinner. I gave him gifts I'd bought in Philly and a card that read, "2 Things You Will Not Be Getting for Your Birthday, Money and Sex."

When he read the card Douglas laughed then tears started streaming down his face. He said they were tears of joy. No one had done anything that nice for him on his birthday. He loved me so much. He sure wasn't making this easy.

After dinner, Douglas and I lay in bed holding each other. He started kissing me, but it was that time of the month. I decided to give him head, something he'd been seeking for months. It was my first time. I knew it would mean the world to him being my first.
I kissed him from his lips to his belly button as I slowly stroked his dick. He stared at me with a look of excitement. "Is she really about to give me head?" he must've been wondering.

I put his dick in my mouth, sucked it for about 30 seconds and stopped. I didn't know what else I was supposed to do. I was not about to let him cum in my mouth. When I moved back up to kiss him, he said he couldn't believe what I'd just done. It was the best birthday gift ever. He held me and fell asleep. I lay awake in his arms for hours, staring into space. How was I going to break up with him after that?

I shook Douglas lightly and told him we needed to talk. I could no longer deal with his insecurities, I said, and we could only be friends. He looked at me in disbelief. His silence spoke volumes. Tears followed.

"Why Amarie? You know I love you more than anything in the world. Why? What type of person are you to make me feel so loved and then tear my world apart?" I felt horrible, but I had to stick to my guns.

I started dating Ralph a few weeks later. Douglas called while we were at breakfast. I told him I couldn't talk. He begged me to listen. I gave him a few minutes but I didn't want to be rude to Ralph. Douglas was crushed. He called and texted me every day for months. Every year he would call on his birthday to remind me how much I hurt him and forced him to move up north. He couldn't live in Florida knowing I was just a drive away and he couldn't see or touch me.

I felt guilty each time I spoke to Douglas. I thought I was giving him good memories by going all out for him on his birthday. He didn't see it that way.

Tips for the Ladies: Insecurity isn't sexy on women or men. If your man is insecure, it's not you, it's him. There's nothing you can do to help. If you can't deal, cut him loose. But make a clean break. Don't drag it out. (And please don't treat him like a king and sex him first!) It will only hurt more in the end.

Tips for the Fellas: If you have a woman who is giving you the attention, loyalty and respect you deserve, despite your situation, hold on to her. Don't push her away with your insecurities. She obviously sees something in you. Your job is to find confidence so you can see it, too. If you can't, date someone at your level. It will better for your ego and your relationship.

DEAD BEAT

I met Marvin at a birthday party. He had a female roommate whom he said I probably knew as we were involved with similar community groups but he never told me her name. Marvin texted me right before our first date asking if he could get some. "Some what?" I asked. "Some pussy," he responded. Was he for real? I told him I wasn't ready to get down like that and didn't hear from Marvin again for weeks. When he finally called, I told him I wasn't interested.

Six months later, I learned the identity of Marvin's roommate. Patricia and I had started doing business together when I found out she was Marvin's live-in girlfriend. Over time, I witnessed the ups and downs of their relationship. He couldn't keep a job, had no car, depended on Patricia financially and had no involvement in his children's lives. He had mental and emotional issues, and he cheated on Patricia. He was a deadbeat who knew Patricia would always clean up his mess.

Not only did Patricia deserve better, she needed to stop enabling Marvin so he would grow up. I was grateful I hadn't gotten involved with him.

Patricia said she stayed in the relationship because she loved Marvin and he needed her. She did eventually end things, move back home and became happy as a result.
Marvin continued to live the same life with a different woman.

Tips for the Ladies: Love won't make a man grow up. Holding him accountable will. Men want women who will force them to Man Up. They don't respect and will take advantage of women who put up with their shit and take care of them despite their deadbeat ways.

Be supportive, loyal and loving to a man who puts in the work to be the best man, father and partner he can be. A man who respects and appreciates you.

Tips for the Fellas: Your woman is not your mother. Man Up and take responsibility for your actions. Do a self-evaluation. How are you contributing to the relationship? What can you do to lighten the load and contribute to your woman's happiness? If you truly care for her, uplift her by doing your part financially, emotionally, and by showing her the utmost respect.

NEAR DEATH

Not long after Alicia, one of my best friends, moved back to town she began dating Ike.

They became pretty serious really quickly. I would overhear disturbing conversations between them and she would share equally disturbing text and voice messages from Ike.
"Where the fuck you at?" he'd say. "Why aren't you answering your fucking phone?" "I'm outside your door and if you do not open the door, I am going to kill myself."

I told Alicia he seemed crazy and his language was unacceptable. Still, she kept seeing Ike.

They moved in together and she got pregnant. Ike denied the baby and started disrespecting her even more. Alicia finally broke it off and asked him to move out. After their daughter was born, though, she gave him another chance. They moved into another apartment. Ike started physically abusing her. Despite the involvement of law enforcement, she never pressed charges.

She kicked him out again but on a visit with their daughter he stole Alicia's keys. She thought the baby misplaced them. A month later, Alicia denied a request from Ike to stop by because she was going out with a friend. When he asked whether her companion was male or female she told him none of his business.

It was a man and Alicia brought him home. As they sat in her apartment talking, she heard the door unlock. Ike came in waving a gun. The man left when Ike threatened him. Ike then started beating

Alicia in the face with the gun. He kicked and punched her. He threatened to kill her for going out with another man. He held her down and put a gun in her vagina.

When he left Alicia bleeding on the floor for a brief moment, she grabbed her cell phone and called 911. He returned and resumed beating her as she lie on the floor defenseless. Ike continued hitting her even after the police arrived. They had to taze him several times.

If Alicia had not gotten that window to call 911, she most likely would be dead. It took weeks for the swelling to go down on her body and months before she could sleep without fear. She loved him but hated what he had done to her. He nearly took her from her children. She pressed charges and sent him to prison for attempted murder.

Ike was one of the finest underclassmen during my senior year in high school. A few months before he and Alicia started dating, I'd run into him while visiting the family of a deceased classmate. We exchanged numbers but he attended the services with another woman and ignored me. I deleted his number.

What would have happened had he spoken to me at the funeral? Or had I reached out to him? I thank God I will never know. Still, I feel Alicia's pain. I wouldn't want any woman to experience what she went through.

Tips for the Ladies: Pay attention to the signs. Abuse usually starts out verbal. A man who disrespects you with his tongue will dishonor you with his fists. No form of abuse is acceptable - verbal, emotional, mental or physical. Love does not hurt. We all will experience a broken heart. But no one should break your bones or spirit. Get out at the first sign of abuse. If you don't, you may not live to talk about it.

Tips for the Fellas: If you have thoughts of abusing a woman or are already engaged in abusive behavior, get help. You have a problem and need therapy. Violence is never acceptable.

BABY MAMAS ON STEROIDS

Danny was a star college football player when I was a high school sophomore. He played overseas after messing up his chance to play in the NFL. His siblings and I were classmates and good friends so I'd see Danny on his visits home and we'd flirt. Once, he gave me a picture to remember him by. This, of course, was before Facebook.

One night, my girl Sonya and I were kicking it at a club when I ran into Danny's younger brother. He told me Danny was back in South Florida and working at the club. I told him to tell him I said, "Hello," if he remembered me. I'd run across Danny's picture a couple of weeks earlier as I was searching albums for a picture to use as a goal to reclaim my sexy.

As my girls and I were taking a picture with the club photographer, I noticed a guy in the area sucking the air from the fan. As we waited for our picture to be printed, he came over.

Danny: Are you from around here?
Me: Yes.
Danny: Are you single?
Me: Maybe.
Danny: Can I get to know you?
Me: You already do.
Danny: What? How?

I explained that I hung out with his siblings. He remembered. We talked briefly and then we exchanged numbers. I told Danny I'd see him around as I went back to the dance floor.

He called me and invited me to breakfast shortly after I'd gotten home.

"Should I pick you up?" he asked. "No," I replied, "I will meet you there."

It had been over 13 years. He could be a stalker or crazy. He was not going to know where I lived.

At breakfast I learned that Danny had seven children, two 18-year-olds, two 16-year-olds and the others 12, 11, and 4. "Wow!" I thought. "Two sets of twins, huh?"

"No," said Danny. "All individuals, from seven different women and from all different cities and states."

"Damn you are fertile!" I said laughing out loud. "I might get pregnant just eating breakfast with you."

Danny didn't think I was funny. My bad. But he did have baby mamas on steroids.

Danny was a rollin' stone. Wherever he laid his hat was his home.

He explained that women liked football players so he gave them what they wanted.

He tried to convince me that he was a changed man and didn't roll like that anymore. He wanted to try to get to know me better and see where it could lead.

He claimed that his last girlfriend cleaned out his bank account, supposedly over $70,000. So he moved back to South Florida to his mother's house and was working three jobs.

On a positive note, he was studying Information Technology.

But he also was paying child support for five of his children. No wonder he had to work three jobs.

That was an earful but I was happy that Danny was honest and upfront. The thought of being baby mama number eight, dealing with loads of child support and potential baby mama drama, though, was too much. Plus he was trying to rebuild his life on top of all that. It was not an attractive situation.

He had nothing to show for his years of success as a football player. He was too old to start over. Where would that leave me? Sure he was trying to improve his situation but I wasn't trying to be Captain Save a Man. Plus I didn't know what else he was spreading other than his seeds. I had to let Danny boy know I wasn't interested in being anything but friends.

Tips for the Ladies: If you are single, have no kids, and want kids, run away from a man like Danny unless you want to struggle financially. If you end up getting married you will have the burden of his child support payments and his baby mama drama.

Tips for the Fellas: Wrap It Up! Just because the women want "A Baller" doesn't mean you have to give them baby ballers. Women will overlook one or two baby mamas but multiple children with multiple women in multiple locations is just irresponsible. No woman wants that kind of responsibility or drama. Plus you have no resources left for her.

DATE FROM HELL

It was 2004 and South Florida had three back to back hurricanes. Winds roar, rain beats loudly against the roof, windows and doors. Lightning seems only a few yards away when it strikes.

You lie still and pray quietly that it passes quickly. Or you sit bored for hours gazing at your family members. No television, lights or internet. Only a cell phone.

By the third storm, I couldn't take talking to my family anymore. I remembered a commercial for VibeLine, a service that allows strangers to meet over the phone. There had to be other people thinking like me.

One particular guy caught my attention. His voice was strong yet sexy. Tavaris was 26. He described himself as 5'11" with a medium build. We entered a private chat and talked for about an hour before exchanging numbers and agreeing to keep in touch.

Over the next few weeks we talked several times. He said he was an auditor. After the third week or so of chatting, Tavaris asked me on a date. Two days before we were set to meet, he asked if I would pick him up because his car was in the shop. He lived 45 minutes away but I agreed to do the driving.

That morning, I woke up excited and nervous. No matter what, I had to be fly. I went to the mall and bought the cutest burnt orange shirt, jeans that made my butt look big and a pair of three-inch heel sandals. I got a mani and pedi and had my eyebrows arched. My hair was already braided so no need for a new do. I jammed to my girl

Mary J. Blige all the way down.

The apartment complex was a little run down but I tried not to be judgmental. As I waited for Tavaris, my stomach tightened. I felt like something was going to go wrong but I ignored the feeling. Tavaris showed up with a doo rag on his head and a mouth full of gold teeth - top and bottom. He was wearing a burnt orange, long sleeve t-shirt and baggy blue jeans with sneakers. He was not the clean cut guy I expected at all. Again, I tried not to be judgmental. Tavaris got in the car and I gave him a hug. I asked what he had planned. He said we would go to the movies to see Get Rich or Die Trying. He didn't know the start time but suggested we would go to the drive-in. That was cool. I hadn't been to a drive-in in ages.

About a mile into the drive, Tavaris asked me to pull into a bar so we could have a drink. There were very few people there. I assumed it was still early. He ordered us drinks. We talked for a few minutes before a couple approached. They asked if we were a couple and remarked how cute it was that we dressed alike. We explained that we were not yet a couple and hadn't planned to wear the same colors.

Tavaris suggested we play video games.

We played a couple of minutes before he gave me his tokens and left, saying he'd be back in a few minutes. I played for about five more minutes before returning to the bar.
Ten more minutes went by and still no Tavaris. I looked around and even asked a guy to check for him in the men's room. Tavaris was nowhere in sight.
My temper started to flare. No this fool has not left me in this strange bar by myself.

I grabbed my keys and headed outside. I ran into Tavaris walking from across the street with the couple whom we'd met earlier.

"I am leaving!" I told Tavaris. "How dare you leave me in an unfamiliar bar by myself?"

He stopped me. He explained that he'd gone across the street to get some paper. What kind of paper? I asked. He didn't respond, got in the car and told me to head to the movie.

Still pissed but hopeful the night would get better, I drove towards the drive-in. The movie had begun an hour before we arrived. By then I was truly pissed. I told him I'd take him home and be on my way. Tavaris insisted that we try a theatre on Las Olas Boulevard in downtown Fort Lauderdale.

I agreed. I asked Tavaris about his gold teeth. They were removable, he said. He had made a conscious decision to wear them that night. He took them out and put them back in as proof.

All of the movies at the Las Olas Theater had begun playing already. Tavaris suggested we go dancing and led me to a nearby club. They were jamming dancehall reggae so I figured it'd be cool.

Tavaris handed the bouncer something I couldn't identify. The bouncer signaled the girl at the door to let us in. At our table, he pulled a bag of weed and the "paper" from his pocket. My mouth fell open and my eyes widened. "What the hell are you doing?" I demanded. "Is that what you got paper for? Did you get that from the couple? Oh hell no, I'm getting out of here! You are about to get us arrested and I am not going to jail for nobody!"

Tavaris asked me to calm down, saying he had already taken care of security. I snatched my purse, left the club and headed to my car.

Tavaris ran behind, yelling my name. He caught up, grabbing my hand to stop me.

"Look, I know this has not been the best first date and I'm sorry," he said. "I promise I will make it up if you let me. Let's just walk over here by the water and sit and talk for a minute. I promise it will get better."

A part of me wanted to keep walking to my car. The other part said give him one more chance.

We walked to a bench by the water where we sat and talked for about thirty minutes. Tavaris noticed a closed water taxi with a "No Trespassing" sign. He suggested we be daring and get on. I pointed out the sign and the fact that I couldn't swim. He convinced me anyway.

We climbed on to the water taxi, laughing. When a security guard passed with his flashlight we ducked. After he passed, I said we should get off. Tavaris had something different in mind. "I can make you feel good on this water taxi," he said, "by tasting you and licking you all over." I had no idea how the hell we got from having a horrible date to sneaking on a water taxi to him licking me all over.

I told Tavaris that as tempting as that sounded, I would have to pass and I suggested we leave. He begged me over and over again. I was not in the mood for that; not to mention the possibility of being caught for indecent exposure. I was not trying to have my face on a police blotter, especially not for him.

As I headed back to Tavaris' apartment, he told me his cousin lived at the place where I'd picked him up. He was going home, which was in another location. We stopped at what I believed was his apartment only to find out it was another cousin's place. He'd left his key there. Tavaris asked me to go up to the apartment with him. It appeared to have suffered severe damage from the hurricanes. Inside it was dark and moldy. We entered his cousin's apartment. The lights weren't working. It was pretty scary.

Tavaris fumbled in the dark in search of his "key." He then proceeded to a room with light shining in from the outside lamp post. He took a seat on a moldy looking couch and asked me to sit next to him. "Tavaris, I am ready to go home. It has been a long night and I do not want to come and sit by you on that raggedy couch."

Tavaris told me I thought I was all that and had been acting bougie all night. The lady in me went out the window. "I am all that you bitch ass nigga!" I yelled. "Fuck you and lose my goddamn number."
What the hell was I thinking to put myself through that torture as if it was really going to get better? I should have left his ass at the damn bar.

Tips for the Ladies: Always ride in separate cars on a first date with a man you've never met. First and foremost, it's smart to be safe. Second, you can leave whenever you want. Also, listen to your gut. It is usually right. If it tells you something isn't right go with that. Don't be afraid to walk out on a date your gut is telling you will go badly. Hurting a man's feelings should be the least of your worries.

Tips for the Fellas: This is not the way to impress a lady. Show your date the respect and consideration of having a plan for the time she's willing to invest with you. Winging it is unacceptable. If you smoke weed or indulge in other illegal activities warn your date ahead of time and let her choose whether she wants to be involved.

Anything less is just tacky. Also, you'll know if you're getting some. Women are good at giving hints. You won't have to beg. It's best, though, to just assume you're not getting any on a first date.

WTF? YOU DIDN'T MARRY ME!

I had a bachelor's from FAMU, an MBA from Nova Southeastern University and I was president and CEO of a successful boutique public relations firm at 24. By 26, I'd bought a brand new townhome. What more could a girl ask for? Someone special to share my life with. Of all the men I'd dated, I had yet to find myself in a committed, long term relationship.

I did a relationship assessment. I realized I had pushed away all the guys who wanted a serious relationship with me because I was afraid of commitment and focused on my career. The other guys I'd dated were just friends with benefits.

I had to make a change to experience something different, something real. I wanted to fall in love like never before and have someone truly love me. I wanted a true commitment. I prayed that God would send me a man who would love and accept me for me. And I would love and care for him. I made a promise to myself and God that I would have an open mind, would treat him right and do everything in my power to make it work and not hurt him. Amen.

I was updating my MySpace profile one day when I decided to see who was online locally. I saw a few lame profiles but just as I was about to log off, I came across a picture of a man lifting weights. He had nice abs and wasn't bad looking. While browsing through his pictures, I noticed his paintings. They were beautiful and vibrant. His talent drew me. I sent a message telling him so.

His name was Shelton and he had recently moved to Florida from California. After three weeks of exchanging emails, he invited me to a movie.

I knew he was Jamaican and I guess subconsciously I wanted to show him I was Jamaican, too. I decided to wear what I now call my "reggae outfit." A black, one-piece halter-top romper with Rasta colors, black sandals and my Rasta "nuff respect" bracelet. I knew I was cute.

He was 6'1", dark, bald and had a killer smile. He wore nice jeans, a fitted shirt and chain belt. He had a gay aura that unnerved me but I did say I was going to be open and not judge appearances.

We smiled and embraced. Our movie didn't start for an hour so we went for drinks.

I ran into a Delta Sigma Theta soror who invited us to join her and her date. We sat and talked with them for a few minutes before taking to the dance floor. Shelton was a good dancer and before we knew it the time had come for the movie.

I had a great time but didn't feel much chemistry. I didn't care if I saw Shelton again or not.

Over the next couple weeks we spoke briefly online and by phone. The next time Shelton asked me out I'd also gotten invitations from two guys I'd met at nightspots. I told my business partner I was on a roll. Three invites in one day!

She told me a Bible story about feast or famine - that I still do not understand – and said I needed to choose one guy. "But why?" I asked. "I am just starting to have fun and explore my options." She gave me a look. "OK, AMarie."
I decided to evaluate each man. One had shallow conversation and was always hanging out in some unsavory neighborhood when

we spoke. Another seemed to only have sex on his mind and had no charm or finesse. We had yet to go on a date and he'd already asked my favorite position. Then there was Shelton. He at least had stimulating conversation.

We met for lunch, then dinner and from there became almost inseparable. I invited Shelton to various events to see how he'd interact with my friends and colleagues. He got along fine with everyone. He introduced me to his friends and I got along with them.

About a month in, Shelton asked if I was seeing anyone else. I told him I wasn't seeing anyone seriously. Truth is, I wasn't seeing anyone at all. "What does it matter to you?" I asked. "It's not like you are my man."

"What are we doing then?" he asked. I was at a loss for words. He asked what I wanted. Again, I was speechless. Shelton asked if I wanted to marry and have children. Of course I did, I told him. He said he wanted the same. We agreed to pursue a relationship. AMarie officially had a man!

For the next three months, Shelton and I spent every evening and free moment together. We went to the movies, car shows, plays, nightclubs and more. And the sex was amazing. He had a great package! We did it two to three times a day on weekends and just about every night or early morning during the week. We could not get enough of each other. Shelton knew all the right places to touch and taste. He had all the right moves. There was never a dull moment.

Shelton was not only great in bed; he was great in the kitchen. He loved to cook and entertain his friends. He must have known that the way to my heart was through my stomach. He made the best curry goat, curry chicken, sweet and sour chicken, peanut porridge and steak and potatoes.

We met each other's family. When his mom came from Jamaica to visit we cooked her a wonderful dinner. She loved me immediately. Every moment with Shelton was filled with excitement and anticipation for what was to come.

One evening Shelton and I discussed the possibility of my getting pregnant. I wasn't on the pill and had no health insurance so our only protection was wrapping it up. He asked what I would do if I got the flu or injured. I told him I'd have to go to the emergency room. He decided to add me to his insurance plan. That was the sweetest thing any man had done for me. I knew then Shelton was serious about our relationship.

About a month later, Shelton said he felt I was maintaining a wall. He wanted me to open up to him more. One evening at dinner, he said he'd never fallen for a woman so fast. He accepted me, he said, unconditionally. I didn't know what to make of his statement. I told Shelton I wasn't sure if I was ready to accept him unconditionally. I didn't want to set myself up to be lied to or cheated on. He was hurt by my honesty.

About a week later, I was at Shelton's apartment when a woman called. "Why are you not answering my calls," she asked. "I came by and you were not home. Why are you doing me like this?" Shelton went outside to finish the call.

I didn't know what to do. Should I leave or should I stay? I went outside to leave but then decided to sit by the pool and think it through. Shelton came over and asked if I had come out to look for him. "No. I was going to leave."

He asked why.

"I do not care who that was and I am only saying this once," I said. "I do not do drama. I do not play games. And I do not share. If you want to be with me then it has to be only me. I am not putting up with any other females because there is too much shit floating around these days and I love me and my health. So let me know right now if you are ready to be with me. If not, I understand and I will go."

Shelton pulled me close, stared in my eyes and said, "That was someone I was seeing when I met you. I have not been with her since we met and I told her I have a woman now. I want to be with you and you only."

A couple of days later, he asked if I loved him. Again, I was caught off guard and had no words. I told Shelton I was not sure and asked if he loved me. He said he'd fallen in love with me. My heart melted.

For the next week, I pondered Shelton's words. I dug deep inside and I found a bit of fear. I didn't know what I was about to get into. Is this what I had asked God for just five months earlier? What I knew is that I felt a strong connection with Shelton that I had never felt before. He hadn't gone to college and wasn't a doctor, lawyer or the type of educated man I dreamed of marrying, but he was smart, talented, artistic, handsome, sexy, funny, and ambitious. He had great potential. The sex was the bomb and he could cook his ass off. Most of all, he loved me. What more could I ask for? I decided to bring the walls down and take a leap of faith. I was ready to love this man named Shelton.

As I prepared to go on a two week vacation to Jamaica that I had planned with my family before Shelton came into my life, I decided to tell Shelton I loved him. One morning as he was leaving for work and reached over to kiss me on the forehead, I looked into his eyes and said, "I love you." He was surprised and smiled the warmest smile as he kissed my lips. "I love you, too," he said.

I knew my trip was going to be the longest vacation ever. The night before leaving, I surprised Shelton with a candlelight dinner, old school soft music, red lingerie, stilettos and the best love making he had ever experienced. Or at least I would like to think. Shelton asked if I had to go. I did. He asked if I wanted to marry him the next morning before I left.

I was in shock. Marriage already?
I told Shelton I didn't want to rush things. No need to worry. I was coming back to him. I fell asleep in his arms to Alicia Keys singing, "Like You'll Never See Me Again," thinking life couldn't get any better. Thank you God for answering my prayer.

I returned from Jamaica right after the start of the New Year. Since Shelton had proposed before I left, I thought it was a good time to discuss our future. Shelton wanted to paint and sell his artwork full time. I was excited for him and decided to support making his dreams come true. I developed Shelton's website, wrote his artist bio and booked him for several exhibitions. Within a few months, he was on a roll.

We decided to save money by moving into together after about seven months since we were spending every night at each other's place. Shelton was hesitant. He'd promised himself he wouldn't move in with another woman unless it was a home he'd purchased or rented with his wife. I owned my townhome already, I told him. Besides, what was mine was now his, too.

When Shelton moved in we were in perfect harmony. We cooked and watched TV together and shared household chores. I watched him paint. He watched me work. It was heavenly. We decided to hold off on marriage and live together for a year to see how things would work. We got a joint bank account and named each other as secondary beneficiaries to our life insurance policies. We were building an exciting future.

Months had gone by when our friends started to complain about not seeing us. I told my girls I would make time for them, but they needed to understand I was adjusting to my relationship. Shelton, on the other hand, started going out three to four nights a week. We all need space, but this was drastic. Slowly, I began to see a change in Shelton.

Shelton had never been into his cell phone. His family and friends always complained about him never answering it. He would leave it in every room of the house and never bothered searching for it once he got home. Suddenly, Shelton was attached to his phone like a Siamese twin. It began ringing all hours of the night. The first time, I told Shelton to tell whoever was calling to not call him after 11. I tried not to trip. The calls, though, didn't stop.

One morning while Shelton was in the shower, I searched his phone. I found text messages from the chick he was dating when we met saying that she missed him. She knew he had a girl but still wanted to see him. She invited him to Naples. There also were messages between Shelton and chicks he had met in the club.

When Shelton came out of the bathroom, I confronted him. He was pissed that I had searched his phone but I didn't care. I reminded him that I didn't share and told him to cut the mess. When he left for work I called the ex-girl to properly introduce myself. She called me a bitch and said she was not going to stop calling Shelton until he told her to stop. This bitch had some fucking nerve!

I had never searched a phone or called another chick. This was out of character for me.

I called Shelton at work and told him what she said. He already knew because she was on his other line. Shelton saw nothing wrong with talking to his ex-girlfriends as long as he wasn't "fucking them." He didn't see anything wrong with making new female friends at clubs or the job as long as he wasn't "fucking them." This was the beginning of our rocky road ahead.

I continued to support Shelton's art. I wanted us to have a successful and meaningful life together and I was willing to go through ups and downs. Over the next six months, there were far more downs than ups. But I was lost in love. So lost that that I overlooked what was happening around me in order to make the relationship work.

The Great Recession started and the U.S. economy took a dive, taking with it my business revenue, property value and Shelton's hours at work. Things were tight.

Shelton wanted me to do my business on the side and get a full time job while he continued to work his one job with fewer hours. I agreed to get a part-time job if he would get another part-time job. I became frugal and would only buy what we needed. Shelton would use our bill money to buy clothes, shoes and electronics that were way out of our budget. He would hide the things be bought in the closet, under the bed, in the trunk of the car and even in the cars of our friends and family. I'd get angry, hurt and lash out. He could've at least bought me something. Shelton was selfish and irresponsible.

But that wasn't the half of it.
Shelton bought a plane ticket to Jamaica without telling me at a time when we had no money. I had just started to work for the Barack Obama presidential campaign. I found out about his trip reading a text message to his friend in Jamaica. He told her not tell me. I played it cool. When a letter came notifying Shelton he had a reception for an art exhibit the same evening he was scheduled to fly to Jamaica I called and politely told him he would need to change his flight. Shocked that I knew, he had nothing to say so I just hung up on him.

The day before his trip to Jamaica, Shelton spent almost all of the money I made from the campaign on gifts for his family and friends in Jamaica. He said he would send it back to me once he got there. I knew that wasn't going to happen. He missed his return flight, costing me another $200. I was pissed but I kept telling myself we would get past this bad patch. We would be alright.

While checking Shelton's inbox for messages about his art, I came across an email from a girl he'd met in Jamaica. She enjoyed meeting him and as they were dancing in the club she thought about the things she wanted to do to him. I brushed it off.

About a month later, Shelton and I were sending a proposal to a potential client when I noticed a message titled, "My Trip to Florida" from the same woman. "Shelton, what the hell is this?" I asked. He quickly tried to close my laptop and take it from my hand. We began a tug of war. I would not back down.

Finally, he stopped fighting over the laptop and left the room.
The woman was planning to pay Shelton a visit and wanted to know his favorite color, favorite food and the kind of clothes she should bring. She thanked him for making her hotel and rental car reservations and was excited about their upcoming weekend together. Shelton wrote that he, too, was excited. She noted that she didn't want to leave him voicemails because she didn't want his girl to hear them and get upset. He told her not to worry because he was buying a phone that he could lock. My stomach sank. I could not believe this was happening to me, to us. What was going so wrong in our relationship?

I stormed out of the room and demanded an explanation. I told him to pack his things and leave. Shelton put his arms around me, apologized and promised to stop communicating with her. He sent her an email. "My girl knows about us," he wrote, "so we must end all communications." Deep down, I knew he wasn't done with her.
I confided in one of my male friends who advised me to put Shelton out for a week or two to show him I was serious. He said that if I didn't do it, things would only get worse. Shelton would believe he could get away with anything.

I did not follow my friend's advice. I was afraid Shelton would leave and never come back.

Two weeks later, Shelton got an iPhone. I was angry that he hadn't consulted me about this $300 purchase that increased our phone bill from $55 a month to more than $200. Shelton, of course, saw nothing wrong. "His money" paid for the phone. I let the lights get turned off since I had none of his money to pay the bill. After a couple days without electricity, though, I had it turned back on because I was the one suffering.

One night, Shelton was looking at the pictures he'd taken with his new phone so I asked to see them. He must've forgotten about the photos he'd taken of his dick. He hadn't sent them to brighten my damn day so I wanted to find out who he'd sent them to.

Turned out he was sending the dick pics to the girl in Jamaica. And she was sending him pictures of her pussy. She couldn't wait to have him inside of her.

This was some bullshit! I sent the two of them a message.

"I know you are still communicating. Shelton, you need to find somewhere else to live because I am done. Ms. Insatiable, you are a desperate bitch that would fly all the way to Florida to look for a man that has a woman. You probably have AIDS and are spreading it wherever you can, you nasty whore. You better find him a place to live since you were coming to take care of him. His broke ass does not have any money. You two motherfuckers have a great life together!"

Then I called Shelton and cursed him out. The chick was next. She had the nerve to tell me, "You must be a young bitch to be calling me. Your man is going to fuck who he wants to and I am going to fuck who I want to. I do not give a fuck about you and neither does any other bitch."

"Wow, I guess you are right, bitch" was all I could think to say.

Over the next five months, Shelton and I grew more distant. The closer I tried to get to him, the more he pulled away. He moved his brother in with less than a day's notice. Then he moved his friend in with less than a week's notice. Shelton thought he was on top of the world. He had received lots of publicity from the promotions I did of his artwork but he forgot about the role I played. Us became I and we became me. He acted as if he had done it all on his own. He told me he needed space and that I needed to lose weight because he had become less attracted to me. My self-esteem began to dwindle. I had never had esteem issues in my life. We stopped talking about marriage. Where was the man who I'd thought I would spend the rest of my life with and have beautiful babies? The man I'd centered my whole life my around? I was miserable.

Whenever Shelton would come home or I felt the need to speak to him my stomach would knot. I'd get nauseous and experience shortness of breath. I began having anxiety attacks. Shelton showed me no affection. We had sex once a month if that. When I mentioned it, he'd say I was too horny, he was tired or not in the mood. I felt unloved and unattractive.

One evening, his brother and I were watching television when he asked, "Where is Shelton?" I told him that I had been trying to reach him all day but hadn't heard back. Moments earlier, though, I'd seen pictures on Facebook of Shelton on a cruise with girls. His brother shook his head. "He is on a cruise without his woman and didn't call and tell you or answer your call?" Then his brother stated what should have been obvious. "Ann Marie, he is not in love with you. A man who is in love would not treat you the way he does."

My heart was broken. My life seemed shattered to pieces. My knight in shining armor had turned into my worst nightmare.

I knew things had to change, but I did not know how. We had defaulted on my mortgage in an effort to get a loan modification. I had used all my savings to buy a car since mine had died. I was afraid of what would happen to me financially. I had become dependent on two incomes and business was not going well. We grew more and more apart.

One day I noticed that Shelton had changed his Facebook status to single. I confronted him about it when he came home. I told him if he wanted to be single he should get gone. He shook me violently. I could not believe he had put his hands on me that way. When he finally let me go, he said he was going to move out before one of us killed the other.

I knew he'd been searching for an apartment that he claimed was for us if we got the modification and rented out the townhouse, but I knew it was a lie. He'd also opened a new bank account. Shelton had been planning his escape for a while.

Within two weeks, Shelton had found a place. There was nothing I could do or say to change his mind about leaving. Let's get counseling, I said. Let's try to work it out. I will join the gym and give you space. I thought you weren't leaving unless I put you out. Nothing I said mattered. He was moving and that was that.

I spent a few days in Orlando with my college friends who don't know how much it meant that they were there when I needed them. (I love you ladies!). My world was shattered to pieces and I didn't know what to do with myself.

When I returned, Shelton had emptied our bank account. I didn't have money to pay my bills. I was at an all-time low and didn't know where to turn. I had never asked anyone for anything. I always had something for a rainy day, but not this time. God, my family and friends were all I had left. I had to put away my pride to survive but I made it through.

It took me a while to get past the hurt and pain Shelton caused. I blamed myself for what seemed like a failed relationship. My self-esteem was at the lowest of the low. The last thing I wanted to do was date again. I didn't think I could love again. I had to pray long and hard that God would take away any bitterness. I did not want the next man to pay for what Shelton had done.

Shelton, though, wasted no time. He acted as if we were never an item. Within a year of our breakup, he had been in at least three relationships and had gotten married and had a child with a woman he knew four months. "What the Fuck?" I thought. "He didn't marry me after all the shit I did for him and went through!"

I realized, though, that it was best we hadn't married. I was not perfect in the relationship but I was loving, faithful, supportive, forgiving, loyal, selfless and ready to do whatever it took to build a life with Shelton. He was unappreciative and not ready for a woman like me.

Tips for the Ladies: Don't let love blind you to a man's faults or cheating ways. And recognize that self-esteem comes from inside, not outside. A man can't take your self-esteem unless you give him the power. Only a desperate woman puts up with lying and cheating and tells herself things will get better if she does something different. Don't lose your identity in a relationship. You should always be your number one priority.

When a man shows you who he is believe him and act accordingly. A man who doesn't manage money well shouldn't have access to yours. A man willing to share his time and affection with other women shouldn't have access to yours.

We blame a lot of things on love. But remember you are better off loving some people from a distance.

Tips for the Fellas: When you stop being attracted to a woman or she simply stops meeting your needs, leave - don't cheat. You will save her and yourself a lot of pain and drama. Have integrity in your relationships. Clearly, there are many women who don't mind being one in the number. If you are not ready to be committed, don't lie and say you are. Keep it real and get with these women. Leave the women who want to be the one and only alone.

YOU HAVE PICTURE MAIL

Omar had been crushing on me and trying to get my number for more than two years. I finally gave it to him, but he ruined his chances before the first date.

Omar worked at a local meat market - in the literal and figurative sense of the word. We'd seen each other many times. I shopped for meat there often, and with the exception of the day I went with my boyfriend Shelton he asked my for number every time. I always said, "No."

Then I broke up with my boyfriend. It was an emotional period. I was used to shopping for two, buying all of Shelton's favorite foods. I didn't know what I wanted for myself. Omar was attractive compared to the other workers. He also was the youngest; in his mid-thirties. I gave him my number this time. I needed someone to stroke my ego.

He lived about an hour north of me, had one child and "kinda had a girlfriend." I didn't care. I just needed someone to talk to.

During our third conversation, Omar asked if he could come by. I told him I wasn't comfortable with that and suggested he take me out. "What is the difference in going to your house versus going out?" he asked.

Was that a trick question? "My house is more intimate and it is my private space where I only invite someone I am comfortable with at the appropriate time," I said. "Meeting in a public space is open and I will feel safer." He didn't get it so I ended the conversation.

The next day, Omar called and asked to take me out on a day his shift ended early. I agreed and suggested dinner. Then I had a realization. "Are you going to bring a change of clothes and do you have a friend or family member's house to change?" I asked. "After working all day in a meat market, won't you smell like meat?"

He said he planned to shower at my place. This fool thought he was slick.

I told him he couldn't shower at my house.

"You would let me drive all the way home to shower and change," he asked, "drive back to take you out and then drive back home?"

"Yes I would!" I responded. "If you really want to see me, then you will do it."

He said he'd call back later.

I didn't hear from Omar for four days. He sent me a text message that read, "Take me as I am."

What the hell? Was he listening to Mary J. Blige? I asked him what that was supposed to mean.

He called and asked me to take him as he is. Still not knowing what the hell he was talking about, I reminded him that he "kinda had a girlfriend."

He claimed he was only pulling my leg and that if I was looking for a relationship so was he. He didn't want me only for sex.

I reiterated that I wasn't looking for a relationship as I had just came out of one. I wanted to get to know him slowly.

Two days later, Omar sent me a text. "Send me a picture of you."

I looked through all my cute photos on Facebook and sent one. "I look really pretty on this one," I thought. "He should like it!"

Omar texted back, "That's nice, but I didn't mean a pic like that one."

Oh no he didn't! What's wrong with my picture?

Another text came. "I meant one like this..."

No he didn't just send me a naked picture of himself!

Now, don't get me wrong. The brother looked good. But I was not going to send naked pictures of myself to a virtual stranger. "Thank you," I wrote back. "But I do not send intimate pictures of myself over the phone or internet."

Omar said I didn't have to include my face and promised not to show it to anyone.

Oh, hell no! This fool has lost his mind.

"No. I cannot do that. Sorry."

Omar called. "Why won't you send me your picture? I feel so imbalanced. I sent you mine and you won't send yours," he said. "That's like you telling me you love me and I don't say it back. I feel so bad. Please send me your picture so I can feel balanced."

Did this fool just call me and say he feels imbalanced? Wow!

"Omar, I sent you a picture, but it wasn't what you wanted. You decided to send me your naked picture. I did not ask for it. Thank you. It was nice, but inappropriate."

He blew up. "Is this how you play with men's minds?" he asked. "Is this how you play with my feelings? I show you I am interested in you and you play with me!"

"Omar, I... I." Click. He hung up on me.

What the Fuck! This man was officially deemed crazy.

Tips for the Ladies: The men you become interested in only because they are there are not worth your time. You've been ignoring them for a reason.

Tips for the Fellas: Don't show off your goods unless you and the recipient are on the same page and the feeling is mutual or you will be embarrassed. If you do decide to send your package via text without warning don't get mad and act like a little bitch if the woman on the other ends doesn't show you hers. Just tell her you wanted to brighten her day with a little eye candy and work your way into it. She may have a change of heart later.

DON'T WANNA PLAY GAMES

Trina's I'm Single Again was my new theme song. One of my besties and I decided to hang out in Fort Lauderdale for a change of scenery. We rolled into a reggae spot downtown that was packed and all the way live with lots of island men. I had convinced myself that I was not going to date any more Jamaican men, so my only interest was to dance, sip on some Hennessy and have fun.

After about an hour, a tall, brown skinned, clean cut, handsome and casually dressed man walked in. "Hmm, let's see if we make a connection," I thought, "and please don't let him be Jamaican."

We connected on the dance floor. His name was Donovan. Oh lawd, here we go, I thought. That is such a Jamaican name. He was an engineer at the airport. It sounded important, but we were in the club so I did not want to talk about work. As we continued to dance, Seroni's No Games began to play and Donovan started singing it to me. After the song ended, he asked for my number. He had to be at work by six in the morning.

"Don't give me your number if you are going to play games," he said, "because I don't play games." Whoa, was he serious? "You asked me for my number," I said, "so I suspect you are not playing games." He claimed he wasn't. We hugged goodnight.

On my way home, Donovan texted me and asked if I had made it home. I told him I would text him when I did. He called shortly after. I learned he had a girlfriend he was about to leave because after two years, "it's just not working."
That was the first sign he was playing games.

The next day, Donovan asked if he could see me at a reggae show my girl and I were attending in Miami. On our way, he called several times asking how soon I'd be arriving. "Damn, he is really blowing up my phone," I said to my girl. "We just met less than 24 hours ago." I was not trying to be on lockdown and let him put salt in my game at the show. But I was cool with him buying me something to eat and drink so he was going to get hit up for that.

He bought me some food but instead of hanging out with us he returned to his friends. I thought that was strange because most guys would introduce new females to their friends. But I wanted to check out the scenery so whatever.

Not thirty minutes later, Donovan texted me to meet him by the lemonade stand. Then I got another text that read, "I will kill you if you tell her where I am going."

What the hell? When I asked who he was going to kill for telling he looked confused then said he was going to be honest. He was texting his cousin not to tell his girlfriend whom he told he was going to the restroom.

Sign number two of playing games.

"Wow, you are funny dude," I said. "I am going to go back over to my friend because I don't do drama."

He hugged and tried to kiss me.

Slow your roll! This is not even a date. You got me some food and now you want a kiss? NOT! I politely told him I don't kiss in public, especially since he wasn't my man and his woman was there. He said he was going to leave his girl at the end of the month in six days.

Sign number three.

The following week, Donovan called everyday several times a day. The week after that, he wanted to take me out. I invited him to

West Palm Beach. We went out to dinner. He wanted to come by my place. I had a male roommate and wanted to see his reaction since I hadn't told him. He heard a key in the door and in walks a man. Donovan gave me a look that said, "Oh shit, who the hell is this?" My roommate said, "What's up man," and walked up the stairs. I laughed and told Donovan he was my roommate.

After noticing I didn't have a TV downstairs, Donovan asked if we could watch a movie in my room. We watched Law & Order for about ten minutes before he reached over to kiss me. I pulled back. I hadn't been with anyone since my boyfriend Shelton and I had broken up two months earlier. His lips felt so good, though, I kissed him back. I guess this kiss gave him the bright idea he was going to get him some. "Baby, you know I really like you," he whispered. "I think you are so beautiful. Look what your kiss has done to me. I am so hard and horny right now. I am so attracted to you and I am leaving my girlfriend this week." It was supposed to be last week, asshole.
Sign number four.

The sweet talk didn't work. I told Donovan it was getting late and he should go. He tried to kiss me again. This time he was forceful, pushing me on the bed and trying to undress me. I repeatedly told him to stop. I looked him in the eyes and told him if he did not stop I would scream for my roommate, have him whoop his ass and then have him escorted out by the police. He backed off and apologized, claiming he was not going to rape me. I ordered him to leave immediately. Donovan called repeatedly the next several days until I finally answered and said I didn't want to see him again and to lose my number.

Tips for the Ladies: If a guy says when he meets you that he doesn't want to play games he is playing games at hello. If he says he has a girlfriend, things should end right there. Donovan was doing all the wrong things from the beginning but I kept taking his calls. If you're into games, that's fine. Play along with your eyes wide open. If you don't want to get played, don't even let him make the first move.

Tips for the Fellas: Stop lying and playing head games just to get some ass. If you are involved be honest. Let us choose if we want to give you the panties based on the facts. Definitely do not try to physically force sex, you will catch a case. Save yourself from the crime and you won't have to do the time.

FRIENDS WITH BENEFITS

My girlfriend Loretta and I were dining at a beautiful restaurant at the Singer Island Marriott beach resort when I decided to flirt with the host. He was fine, tall and had a drop dead gorgeous smile and extreme muscular build. He looked as if he worked out all day, every day and he was checking me out. "I think he likes you," my girlfriend said.

I had broken up with Shelton three months earlier and my girl was going through a divorce. We joked that it would be OK to be "hoes" once in our lives and have fun. On our way out, I slipped the host my number. He called within two hours, excited I had a given him my number. He kept saying how beautiful I was and how he'd been watching me from the moment I walked in. His name was Boris. We worked out at the same gym but at different times. He invited me to work out with him early one morning. I am not a morning person but I wanted to get in shape and seeing his fine ass was a great motivator.

The sweat running over his god-like body distracted me. I imagined him working up a sweat between the sheets. I pushed myself harder than usual. I didn't want to look like a wimp. The sexual chemistry between us was thick.

Boris drove me home when the friend who had accompanied me had to leave early. We talked up a storm during the five-minute ride. There was an awkward pause as I exited his sexy red mustang. He said he'd love to continue our conversation, so I invited him in.

Boris gave me a few sensual kisses on the way to the door that made chills run down my spine. His feathery lips were warm. His soft hands gently held my face. I noticed the time and had to put out the simmering fire to attend a meeting.

Neither Boris nor I wanted a relationship so we agreed to be friends with benefits. We would hang out, have sex and date other people. A week later, Boris came over with Chinese food. We ate, watched a romantic comedy and it was on.

We took a shower. His body was ripped, eight pack and all. We lathered each other while kissing under the warm water for what seemed like an eternity. We burst into laughter when the water turned cold and got out. Boris dried me and led me to the bed. He grabbed oil from my dresser and gave me a massage. I hadn't been caressed in months. Boy did I need that. He kissed me all over. I kissed and caressed him. My body was overheating. I felt like I was about to explode.

We had hot, steamy, breath-taking sex for the next three hours. He knew exactly where to touch, lick, taste and how to move - fast, slow, long strokes – putting me in positions I'd never experienced. I had multiple orgasms.

We lay in each other's arms for about an hour as our breathing deepened and our heartbeats slowed. We almost drifted into la-la land. He knew the rule, though. No sleeping over. He had to go.

Boris and I talked every day. Eventually, he started asking questions like, "So did you talk to any guys at the gym? Have you talked to your ex-boyfriend?" "What do you think about me so far?"

Why was he asking these questions? We were just friends. It wasn't his business who I talked to and vice versa. We weren't going to discuss emotional stuff like our thoughts and feelings. I told him we shouldn't have those kinds of conversations.

We planned a rendezvous for the following week. Boris did not show up or call. Two days later, he called with the excuse that he had to work his second job as a male dancer in Miami at the last minute. He apologized for not calling. A couple of days passed and Boris didn't text or call. I sent him a text asking if everything was OK. "Nothing is wrong with me," he wrote, "I just need to be alone." I asked if the situation was permanent. He didn't reply. There was no word from him for several days so I deleted his number.

I ran into Boris two months later. We spoke briefly and kept it moving. Later that evening, he called and told me I looked good. "Why haven't I heard from you?" he had the nerve to ask. "First of all, I know I look good. I looked good when you met me and I am doing great!" I said. "Secondly, why didn't I call? You wanted to be alone. Remember?"

He told me he goes through phases all the time during which he doesn't call his friends and family for months. I told him that didn't work for me. It was unacceptable. "Take care," I said. "It was good seeing you."

Tips for the Ladies: Be clear about what you want and stand by it. Don't get confused when a Friend with Benefits acts jealous or has temporary moments of concern. He just wants to see if he has you hooked and can have you when and where he wants. An FWB relationship should be on your terms so you don't end up confused and hurt by something that is supposed to be satisfying and fun.

Tips for the Fellas: Don't start complicating things that should be simple when you are just having fun. There are some women who can have relations without the relationship. When you start asking questions and acting like you are interested in more, it confuses us. Please don't do it. Also, if you need a time out, be upfront. Don't disappear for long periods and resurface thinking you can pick up where you left off. When the benefits go, you go.

DON'T SAY MY NAME

Sometimes I venture out alone to clear my head. On a hot summer night, I needed to get out of the house so I went downtown to have a drink. I met a nice guy named Chris. He bought me a drink and took me to meet his boys. I sat with them for hours and had a blast. They became my new best friends.

After a few months, though, I was only keeping in touch with two of them, Chris and Ray. Ray and I were really cool. We talked every day and he helped me deal with some difficult issues. Chris and I talked every now and then. He had recently gone through a breakup.

One night I called Ray to see what he was doing. He was "getting some action" so I called Chris. He invited me over to watch a movie. Shortly after, my homeboy Frank invited me to play spades with his boys. I decided to go with Frank and invited Chris. Frank picked me up and Chris met us there. We had a great time, despite losing badly.

Chris agreed to drive me home since he lived on the same side of town. He drove past my community. I asked him where he was going and he told me to watch the movie. Now, he could have at least asked me if I still wanted to do that. But I went along since it was the weekend and I didn't have to work in the morning.

I chose Riddick since I love Vin Diesel's fine ass. As I got comfortable next to Chris, he snuck in a kiss. "So you just gone sneak one in huh?" I asked. "I wanted to do that from the time I met you," he said. "I really like you and want to see where this can go."

Here we go, I thought. "If you like me so much," I asked. "How come I rarely talk to you or even see you?" He answered, "Well, I was getting over a situation and so were you and we are here now, so what better time than now?"

I laughed at the game he was trying to run on me. He looked at me puzzled.

"Chris, let's be real. Don't try to give me that sweet talking crap. If you are horny and want some, just say it!" I shocked him speechless. "Chris, are you horny?"

He was honest about that much. "Yes. Hell yes."

"So why do you want to play with my emotions instead of just being upfront?" I asked. He shrugged his shoulders.

"Let's watch the movie."

Five minutes later he kissed me again.

I was horny, too. It had been a while. It's not like I wanted a relationship with him but he might be a good cuddle buddy since I didn't have one.

He kissed me again, caressing and touching me in all the right places. He put on his condom and inserted himself. I moaned. As I moaned louder, I found I had competition.

Chris' moans sounded way too much like mine. They were too feminine. He started calling my name. "Oh, AMarie. AMarie. Oh, AMarie."

He blew my high. Turned me off.

What the hell! He sounded like a girl calling my name. Am I sleeping with a woman?

"Ahhh, Ahhh, AMarie," he continued. Are you serious? I felt like I was in that scene from Waiting to Exhale where Whitney Houston was doing it with the guy growling like an animal. I literally could not move. I stopped participating. I just wanted him to hurry and cum.

Finally it was over! He happily went to sleep as I lie there wondering who I had just had sex with. That was the last time I spoke to Chris. I couldn't face him without thinking about that experience. I didn't want to insult his ego or manhood. He didn't talk like a girl. He had some bass so I didn't know where that she-voice came from. I did know that I didn't want to go through that again.

Tips for the Ladies: Can you have sex with a man that moans more than you and says the things you should be saying? Not me and that's all I have to say about that.

Tips for the Fellas: If we want to hear you moan like a woman, we would sleep with one.

JUST SLIT MY WRIST ALREADY!

I was grooving to the rhythms of one of the best local reggae bands when Carl started to dance behind me. I danced with him on a few songs. As I was leaving, he introduced himself. We chatted and I gave him my number.

The next day, Carl invited me to take a walk by the docks. It was an absolutely beautiful evening. The breeze was nice and cool and the stars were shining bright. Carl wasn't really my type – he was cute but he had plaits - not locks - and was a little rugged.

As Carl told me more about himself the conversation became less interesting by the minute. He was an unemployed truck driver who didn't want to accept any jobs that were not local because he wanted to focus on buying his own truck and starting his own trucking company. Mind you, he had no money saved, no business plan and had not really taken any steps towards his goal.

He had nothing but excuses and negativity. He wouldn't tell me his age or even his birthday. Can you say weirdo?

He talked about how lonely he was and how he wanted a girlfriend, but no one wanted him. He didn't like to go to the movies or do much of anything fun, mostly because he had no money. I had enough. I told him it was getting late and I had to go home.
"So I probably won't see you again right?" he asked pathetically.
"Why would you say that?"
"I don't believe I can have a girl like you."
I smiled and said, "Sure you will see me again."
Of course, I was lying. He cannot have a girl like me. He was depressing

as hell.

I would die from slitting my damn wrist!

Tips for the Ladies: Run from negative men unless you are Captain Save-A-Man. The negative energy could rub off on you.

Tips for the Fellas: Don't dump all of your issues on a woman, especially on the first date. You will scare away most sane women.

SMELLS LIKE DRAMA

I love when guys get my business card and act like they are so interested in working with me but when they call say things like, "You were looking so sexy and beautiful at the event." It was after ten in the evening when I got a text asking, "What are you up to?"

"Who is this?"

He claimed to be a secret admirer I'd met at a play.

"How can I help you?"

He asked if he could come and see me. Now is it just me, or is this dude really bold?

We have never had a conversation, never gone out on a date, only exchanged business cards and he is asking if he can come and see me after ten! What is wrong with this picture?

Of course I told him flat out, "No!"

Within minutes Darrel called. "You looked so beautiful and sexy the other night," he said. "I had to get your contact information."

I thought you were interested in being one of my vendors.

"Yes," he responded, "but I also want to get to know you."

I told Darrel texting me late at night and asking to come over is not getting to know me. I am a lady and he had to come correct or not come at all.

He asked me to the movies. I accepted and ended the conversation.

I called Darrell to tell him I didn't want to go to the theatre he selected but wanted to meet at a nicer one in a central location. He said he wouldn't have a car at movie time and needed to go to a theater closer to his house.

"So you don't have a car?"

"I will have to talk to you about that when I see you."

I told Darrell I was on my way to the gym and would let him know how I was feeling afterwards. I texted him later that I was too tired.

The next day, Darrell called to ask when he could see me. I told him I didn't know. I asked if he had a girlfriend or wife.

"I will have to talk to you about that when I see you."

He added that his mom was coming to town to help him with some things because he'd gotten into trouble and might be deported.

WTF! Deported! Ok, this is too much.

I told Darrell it smelled like he had drama and I don't do drama. I asked how old he was. Twenty.

"Twenty as in 2-0? Are you serious? You can't do nothing for me."

Darrell said I was rude to say that. I wasn't trying to be rude, I was just being real. What could Darrell do for me? What could he bring to the table? He was still wet behind the ears and had drama already. I never engaged in another conversation with Darrell. He eventually stopped calling.

Tips for the Ladies: If it smells like drama, it is. Run! The first clue was the 10 p.m. random text. A sure sign he lacked substance. Pay attention to the little things. On a positive note, at least he was honest and upfront!

Tips for the Fellas: Thanks for being up front and giving us the right to choose. Never stop doing that. However, four words: Get your shit together!

SKUNK MAN

Computer love can have interesting outcomes.

One rainy Friday night, I was home alone trolling on Blackplanet.com when I came across a profile for Sam. I sent him an instant message and we began an intriguing conversation. The brother was deep. It was refreshing.

Sam was a movie critic for an online publication and a visual artist. His reviews and drawings were stimulating. He had recently moved from up North to live with his parents. He was starting over after breaking up with his son's mom. He was unemployed and didn't have a car. He hadn't needed one in New York.

Nevertheless, he had great conversation and knew how to stroke my ego. He would say things like, "I am trying to attract women like you; attractive, intelligent, educated and driven." I was flattered but wondered why he was trying to attract that type of woman when he didn't have his stuff together? He couldn't add to my life or any other woman's. I told him to focus on himself.

Sam was "about" to get a security job and fix his dad's old car, which was all good, but a conversation was still my limit. After about two months, I decided to meet Sam in person. He still didn't have transportation, so I drove forty-five minutes to see him.

He greeted me with a hug. He was tall and had a nice smile, but as I followed him in I noticed something about his walk. There was definitely no physical attraction.

Sam walked past me a few times as I sat on the couch. It hit me! He reminded me of the actor Christopher "Kid" Reid, from the rap duo Kid 'n Play. I'd seen him in the movie Class Act. Sam had a stiffness in his walk that made me want to yell, "Bend your knees, move your arms! You look like a North Korean soldier." I tried to ignore it and not be so shallow but he looked so weird.

We went to get a bite. I had been craving New York pizza and wanted to be considerate about his budget, so I asked him to find a New York pizza spot. I felt a little bad letting him pay since he had not started working but you gotta let a man be a man and treat you like a lady.

Our conversation wasn't as interesting as it had been over the phone. I started planning my exit since I wasn't really into him. We went back to his neighborhood and walked around a lake before grabbing a seat on a bench. It was a nice night to be outside. It would have been nice if I was feeling Sam.

As we sat in silence, I pulled out my cell and turned on Pandora. I shared my favorite playlists. In the middle of Bob Marley's Redemption Song, Sam asked, "What would you say if I asked to kiss you?"
I looked him in the face. "I would say, 'No.'"
I burst into laughter at the look on his face. I know it was mean but his expression was a Kodak moment. He laughed, too. I went back to Pandora.
"Were you serious?" he asked.
"Yes, I do not kiss on the first date." Of course I made exceptions but Sam was not one.
I told him I was getting tired and needed to head home.

Sam ran inside to get me directions. As he came back out, I smelled a strong, oil based scent. I didn't ask. I just thanked him for the evening and gave him a hug good night.

Why did I do that? All I could smell was whatever he was wearing. I started coughing my lungs out. I turned on the air conditioner but that made it worse. I opened the windows and moon roof but it was still bad.

Sam called to see if I made it home. I hadn't. I asked what the hell he had sprayed on. Was he trying to kill me?
"I am so sorry. It is Ralph Lauren Polo Sport," he said. "You don't like it?"
I told him it was too strong and not to do that again.
I literally coughed all the way home. I had to shower to get rid of the smell.

That was not Ralph Lauren Polo Sport. It must've been some cheap Perfumania or parking lot cologne. For a minute, I was scared. I thought, perhaps, Sam put on some type of love potion. I was chilling with him all evening and didn't smell a thing. Why would he wait until the end of the night to spray on cologne that almost killed me? Did he think he was going to get a good night kiss? Skunks spray the enemy and those they fear. Was Sam trying to make me an enemy? It worked!
I never saw Sam again. He called, emailed, and texted. I responded cordially each time but reminded him that the most we could ever be was friends.
"Was it the cologne?"
"That's part of it."

Tips for the Ladies: Keep a face mask and inhaler in your car just in case you need it for a date. You may also need a change of clothes! Sam was nice, but I was just not into him and told him. It is best to be honest and not lead a man on.

Tips for the Fellas: Be careful what and how much you spray on. Your date may have allergies. Wear something light on the first date that does not smell cheap. Most important, do not spray it on at the end of your date. If you did not get a kiss before the cologne, you will not get one afterwards. Don't believe the commercials.

FIRST 48

I met Alex on Facebook after he sent me a friend request. I accepted him because he met the criteria of having at least 10 mutual friends Alex reached out to me after reading my profile, claiming he wanted to inquire about my business services for his company. I told Alex to give me a call. I gave him details about our services and fees. He said he would speak with his business partners and call me back.

Alex called a few hours later. He and his partners decided they would not be able to engage our services but would consider doing so when business picked up.

"Well, I guess since I have talked to you about business I can inquire personally," he said.
"Inquire about what personally?"
He said my Facebook pictures were gorgeous, my profile interesting and he wanted to get to know me better.
He denied using business as an excuse to holler.
"I see you like reggae, who is your favorite artist?" he asked. "What is your favorite food if you could choose between seafood, Italian and others?"
I was working and couldn't go into details so I suggested we talk later. I didn't want to talk about food anyways because I was hungry. Why did I say that?

"Would you like me to bring you something to eat?" he asked.
No, I replied.
Dinner? No, again.
Alex was persistent. "You can take a break to eat. Everybody has to eat."

I caved. It was a free meal. What did I have to lose?

We met at the restaurant. When Alex stepped out of his Chevy Cavalier I thought, "Wow, that's a pretty big guy in that tiny car." He was at least 6'4, 300 pounds.

He greeted me with a hug. I responded by keeping two feet between us.

Alex was tall, light skinned, bald and on the heavy side. I was not attracted. I do not like big guys unless they are the muscular, football player type.

Dinner, though, wouldn't kill me. Besides, I was hungry as hell.

The food was good and the conversation decent but I had to get back to work. I had several deadlines plus there was no chemistry. At least, for me. Alex acted as if he was in love.

He could not stop telling me I was beautiful, ambitious, sexy, smart and funny.

I took his compliments in stride.

He was trying too hard to impress.

On the phone, he was this big time business owner with an arena football team. In reality, he was a security guard and the football team was his side hustle. He lived with his mother, a move he made after breaking up with his ex-girlfriend. For dinner, he flaunted the one-hundred dollar bill he used to pay the check.

Who carries that much cash these days?

Where was his debit or credit card? Did he even have a bank account?

What really took the cake was him saying he wanted to take me on weekend getaways.

Not in that 1996 Cavalier that he was way too big to be driving!

If that wasn't enough, he begged me to stay and walk with him around the shopping plaza as he tried to hold my hand. I politely reiterated that I had a ton of work. It was the truth. By the time I got home, he called and asked if he could see me again. I told him we would have to see. My time was limited.

About two hours later, Alex called again to hear my lovely voice before he went to bed.

The next morning at 6:45, I got a text. "Good morning sexy, have a great day."

OK, that was early but cute. At 9:20, I got a call. "Good morning, how is your day going?"

"Great I'm preparing for a meeting and will have to chat with you later."

It was a busier day than usual. I had overbooked myself until nine that night I told him.

Alex called every two hours as if he wanted play by play updates of my day. When I didn't answer, he'd leave a voicemail and send a text. By 9:30 that night, I made it home tired and hungry. I just wanted to eat my take-out, watch CNN and unwind. I undressed, turned on the TV, sat on my bed and opened what smelled like heaven. As I took the first bite, my damn phone rang.

I figured I'd just tell him I was busy and he'd understand. He asked if I would call him back. Probably not tonight, I told him. I had writing to do. He said he understood and hung up. Cool, that worked. Or so I thought.

By the time I ate, showered and began my first paragraph, the damn phone rang again.

"Yes Alex?"

"What are you doing?"

"I am writing and I really need to concentrate."

"If you promise to call me back, I will let you go."

Was he serious? Let me go? Negro, I can hang up the damn phone! But I wasn't going to be mean.

"Okay, fine."

"You promise?"

"Yes, I promise."

I finished the introduction to my book and figured Alex could give me some feedback.

I read him the introduction, got his input and told him goodnight.

Whew, what a day! Alex had called and texted me over twelve times within 24 hours.

Day two of the First 48.

At 6:46 in the morning I got a text.

"Good morning sexy, hope you have a great day. Can you have lunch with me?"

I looked at it and went back to sleep.

At 9:00 a.m. Alex called and left a message, "Can you have lunch with me today? Give me a call and let me know so I know when to take my break."

At 9:30, I got another text.

"Let me know about lunch luv."

At 10:15, he called. "Are you going to meet me for lunch?"

"No. I told you last night I need to get some work done since I was out all day yesterday. I will have to chat with you later."

At 11:30, he called and left a message, "I'm on my break and was just thinking about you. Call me when you get a chance."

At 12:45, a text. "Hi, can you talk?"

"No, I'm busy right now."

At 1:30, another text. "Do you trust me enough to let me know where you live? I figured if I come see you, I won't pull you away from your work."

Is he serious?

"No I don't trust you, for all I know you could be a stalker. And yes you would be pulling me away from my work. Are you going to entertain yourself?"

At 1:50, a Facebook instant message. "Hi, how is your day?"

I did not respond.

At 2:15, another text. "Can you talk?"

Again, I didn't respond.

At 2:35, Alex called. I did not answer.

At 2:50, a text. "What night will work better for the movies, Friday or Saturday?"

Movies? Who said anything about going to the movies? Still, I did not respond.

At 3:00, another text! "I just wanna take you away, no phone or computer, no work, just you and me."

Oh hell no! That's it!

I turned to my Facebook family for advice. "I need your help fam! What is the acceptable number of times someone can call, text, or instant message you in one day before he/she becomes a bug-a-boo?"

I love my Facebook family because they keep it real. At first, many people thought it was me trying not to bug some guy. So I received messages like, "Girl only call him 2-3 times and if he doesn't respond, don't call anymore." And "Girl, let him pursue you. Don't pursue him." And "If you like him it shouldn't matter, vice versa."

I had to set the record straight and let them know that it wasn't me. It was him blowing me up! Interestingly enough, the tone changed. "Oh no girl. Something might be wrong with him. He sounds desperate." And "Is he fine. Do you like him? If so, it shouldn't matter."

At 3:45, another text.
"Are you still busy?" He must not be on Facebook, I thought.
"We need to talk."
Alex called immediately.
"I am a very busy woman with a tight schedule and cannot afford to sit and talk on the phone or text/IM back and forth all day. I do not mind one or two phone calls and a few texts throughout the day, but you are being excessive and I can't have that."
"Well you don't have to answer. I just call or text you when I want to let you know what I am thinking."
Was he slow? Nothing against slow people but damn!
"Every time you call or text, my phone alerts me and therefore, I am distracted."
Alex apologized and said he would not call as much.

Several days passed and Alex only called and texted me a couple of times each day.
I did not respond. I was too turned off to care. OK, I know I wasn't attracted to him to begin with, but he could have been a cool friend. About two weeks later, Alex sent a Facebook message. "Hey Sexy, I will give you all the space you need so I don't throw you off your work, but I still want to be the man in your life when you have the time for one and when you can get away, so let me be there for you. I had to pick up a second job back at Applebee's where I worked before. I'm going to Tampa Saturday to stay overnight for the Dallas and Tampa game on Sunday, but can I see you maybe tonight for a minute or two so I can see that smile, get a hug and we can talk a little? Give me a call when you're free or send me a text to let me know what's on your mind and how you feel about that. "

I did not respond.

Are you serious? You will not be talking to me!

About a week later, Alex sent me an instant message on Facebook.

"Did you think about my offer?"

I finally responded "I am not interested in you like that, I'm sorry."

"That's fine!" he wrote.

That was the end of Alex.

Tips for the Ladies: If you are not attracted to a man and see no romantic future with him let him know so neither of you wastes your time. Don't give him any glimpses of hope if you know there is none. For example, "I will call you back." You know you don't want to, so just be honest. Also, set boundaries immediately. Let a man know right away when he is calling and texting too much. How often is too often? When it bothers YOU! Finally, free meals come with a price!

Tips for the Fellas: Don't be a bug-a-boo, especially in the first 48 hours! Yes, we like to be chased and we like to know you are interested and are thinking of us, but don't - I repeat DON'T - bug us. We will run away and you might lose any chance at romance you might have had. Call, text, instant message and email in moderation. And, yes, you fine men out there, this applies to you, too. Some of you can also be bug-a-boos.

What is moderation you may ask? Use the rule of three. Three's a charm. Morning, noon and night. Breakfast, lunch and dinner. The three bears, the three little pigs, the Father, Son and Holy Spirit. Reaching out to a woman three times in one day is sufficient.

ALL OF THIS BAGGAGE WITH ME

Raymond and I met while I was waiting at the bar for a friend at a party. The chemistry was intense. As we talked, laughed, and stared into each other's eyes, it felt as if time had stopped and no one else was around. We were lost in each other for more than three hours. Before I knew it, our lips were touching in a soft, sensual way that made my stomach flutter with butterflies. It felt as if I was instantly in love.

My friend finally came over. He'd been there for a while but I was so lost in Raymond I hadn't noticed. We were dancing when I realized it was five in the morning and I needed to get home. He walked me to my car where we talked for another hour. We kissed good morning for so long I lost track. We did not want to leave each other. It was weird but felt good at the same time.

Raymond and I talked several times a day and hooked up at the restaurant where we met almost every day for about a month. It felt like a match made in heaven but we quickly realized it was not.

We had too much baggage. Mine was my break up with Shelton six months earlier. Raymond could tell I wasn't over it. He asked a question about that relationship once and I talked about Shelton more than twenty minutes. I ended up in tears. Raymond thought it would be unfair to him to get serious with me.

Raymond's baggage also was a previous relationship. He'd ended an engagement about five months earlier and still had financial obligations. He had purchased a home that he put in both their names and bought her a Mercedes Benz. And he was extremely bitter.

Raymond traveled frequently for work and his fiancée used his absence to cheat. He'd heard rumors about her messing around but didn't believe them. Then she started missing his calls and cutting them short. He came home early one night and caught her with another man in their home.

When he called off the engagement, she took his $40,000 in savings from their account and left, sticking him with the mortgage, three car payments and a broken heart.

Raymond was honest about not being ready to get seriously involved. He needed to rebuild his life and get out from under his financial obligations. Moreover, he had to regain his dignity and confidence. We agreed our timing was off. We were both hot messes who needed to get ourselves together.

Tips for the Ladies: Baggage can be the death of a new relationship. The first step is determining whether or not you are ready to move on. Sometimes, you don't know if you have healed until something or someone triggers those deep rooted emotions. If you realize you are still hurting, take more time to heal. Also, it's not a good idea to get involved with someone else who has baggage they haven't checked, regardless of your own emotional state.

Tips for the Fellas: The same advice goes for you. You have emotions like we do. We empathize with you when a female has done you wrong and jacked your emotions, ego and finances. Timing is everything. Rebuild yourself before getting seriously involved.

NO ONE CAN EAT JUST ONE

Can you believe a brother kicked me out of his house over salt & vinegar potato chips?

I met Kamar online. I wasn't interested.
He was unemployed and claimed to be suing his previous employer for discrimination. He was bitter about his ex-girlfriend whom he called a "whore" because she left him for the second time to go back to her husband. It was just way too much drama for me in the first conversation, so I did not call him or answer his calls.

Though I vowed to never go on the free dating websites again, four months later I did just that. I chatted online with a guy who seemed cool for about thirty minutes. He asked if he could call. I instant messaged him the digits.

He already had my number. He said we'd talk before and that I had kicked him to the curb after our first conversation.

Oh My God! Not this guy again! I explained that he had too much drama. Kamar said the drama was over and he wanted us to try again.

He kept inviting me over to let him cook dinner for me. I kept telling him he needed to take me out to a public place. One day, he texted, asking about my day. I asked if he had planned our date. Kamar said he wouldn't have money until that Friday and asked if I could pay for the date. I don't believe in paying until after the third date. I told him I'd wait until Friday.

He then suggested I compromise and let him cook dinner for me. He promised lamb chops, mashed potatoes, veggies and a bottle of wine. It sounded good. Kamar insisted he was harmless and just wanted to meet me. I decided to text a couple of friends his name, address and phone number.

I said I would arrive at 7:30. My day did not end until 9:30. I felt bad that he had prepared a great meal and I didn't show up. He had been patiently waiting for me. He insisted that I still stop by so he could meet me even if I didn't stay for dinner. I felt really bad, so I went.

We hugged. There was no aroma to suggest that he'd cooked. "Where are the lamb chops?" "I didn't cook. I didn't think you were really coming over and if I had told you that when you called, you would not have come over."
I left.

The next day, we texted back and forth and Kamar asked me to come by after work. I didn't have any plans and was bored, so I did. Kamar was fiddling with his computer so I ended up dozing for what turned out to be a couple of hours. When I woke up, it was to a conversation about how I should have sex with him. I told him it wasn't going to happen. Kamar seemed frustrated but I couldn't understand why. I told him before I ever stepped foot in his house that it wasn't happening anytime soon.

I told Kamar I was hungry.
"What does that have to do with me?"
I smiled and asked him to pick me up something to eat.
He said he wasn't going anywhere until he left for Miami later that night. I had better get in the kitchen and get something.
This Negro was really rude. What the fuck!
There were three bags of chips, Tostitos, Ruffles, and Lays Salt &

Vinegar. I grabbed my favorite – salt & vinegar. As I sat on his bed and got ready to bite into my first chip, Kamar said, "You could have eaten any other chip except my salt & vinegar."
I laughed and teased him about how great and fresh the chips were.

I joked with him for a few minutes and realized that he was not joking at all. He repeatedly asked me to put his chips back. Finally Kamar said softly, "I am going to have to ask you to leave."
"What! Are you serious? Are you putting me out over some salt & vinegar chips?"
"I am not putting you out about the chips," he said. "I'm getting ready to go to Miami and I'm annoyed so can you leave?"

Shocked and pissed, I grabbed my purse and keys and gave him the peace sign as I walked out. Unfreakin' believable!
Was it the chips or that I refused to have sex with him? Maybe both. I will never know and really don't care. He was a cheap asshole. I deleted his number immediately. I should have followed my instincts and left him on the curb.

Tips for the Ladies: Go with your first mind. If you think a man is suspect you're probably right. If a man asks you to pay for the first date, you shouldn't have ever had a first date. If you catch him in a lie on the first date, make it your last date. Ditto if he's not a gentleman.

Tips for the Fellas: There is nothing attractive about a cheap, rude, stingy and insensitive guy. Get over yourself!

GUARDED HEART

Charles had just ended a relationship so he didn't want one. But he liked me and wanted to get to know me better. I didn't want a relationship, either, but I was fine with taking it slow and getting to know him, too.

I warned Charles that if we became intimate too soon one of three things would happen: 1.) It'd be bad and we'd go our separate ways; 2.) It'd be great and we'd become friends with benefits; or 3.) We'd like it, grow on each other and end up in a relationship. We rolled the dice.

Three months later we were having long phone conversations, texting, instant messaging on Facebook and seeing each other weekly. We often agreed to disagree on various topics and our conversations were getting deeper and more intense. I felt Charles getting closer. His emotions deepening. My feelings, however, were highly guarded. Charles made it clear he didn't want a relationship and I refused to set myself up for emotional failure.

Plus, I was not fond of some of his ways. He had pulled a few no-call-no-shows.

His excuses included working late, going to the gym, falling asleep or forgetting. He didn't get the concept of consideration. He also started asking questions I wasn't comfortable answering. I warned him he might not really want the truth. He kept asking anyway.

"Have you slept with anyone else besides me because I have only been with you since we started talking?"

Can you handle the truth? I thought.

"Yes, Charles."

The silence was so loud I could hear the static normally drowned by the background noise. "I'm going to bed," he finally said. "I will call you tomorrow."

A few moments later, he sent a text thanking me for revealing my true self.

The next day he sent a series of texts and Facebook instant messages. I made it clear that we were not exclusive and reminded him that neither of us wanted a serious relationship. I also told him that I would eventually be pursuing a long term relationship and needed to explore my options with men who wanted the same.

Charles interpreted that as him being disposable. I told him if he wanted to be the only man in my life he had to make it known and step up his game. He began seeking more time but he didn't make clear what he wanted.

"I like you and I want to continue communicating with you," was all he would say.

One evening Charles asked me if I still felt the same and if I wanted to continue seeing him. I responded nonchalantly, "It is up to you." I didn't care. He'd made things too complicated.

I asked him if he felt the same.

"I still like you," he said, "but I used to think about you every five minutes and I found myself falling hard for you and then reality set in. I was naïve and I can be replaced at any time."

I realized he was now trying to protect his feelings. I could relate. I'd been doing the same.

My wall went up the minute Charles said he didn't want a relationship. It hardened when didn't keep his word. And he hadn't let me know his feelings.

I liked him but I was too busy exploring my options to give him my undivided attention.

I told Charles I couldn't allow myself to fall in love with someone until I felt they were really into me and we were compatible. I had to protect my heart, emotions and pride. My heart could not bear pain or disappointments. If I did not protect my heart who else would? "You are only thinking about yourself," Charles said. "While you are protecting your heart, what about the hearts you are protecting it from? They have feelings too."

Tips for the Ladies: It isn't wrong to protect your heart, especially when the man you're dating doesn't give you a reason to let down your guard. Keeping your emotions in check is wise until you see evidence they will be handled with care.

Tips for the Fellas: Be clear about your intentions. Let a woman know exactly what you want with your actions and your words. If you are seeking a serious relationship and want to date exclusively, make it known. Don't assume the woman you are dating is monogamous unless you both have agreed to be. And don't ask questions if you can't handle the truth.

MAKE IT CLAP

Walmart is not the place to find a date. I try to get in and out quickly, especially on weekends. I was doing my monthly shopping in Walmart not really trying to talk to anyone. I was wearing my black yoga pants, a tank top and a hooded sweater with some sneakers. As I listened to my iPod, I noticed a guy who popped up on each aisle I walked down. He was walking toward me with his lips moving. I turned down my iPod. I asked him to repeat himself. He'd been trying to get my attention for a while. I smiled and apologized for not hearing him.

He looked around 22 or so but he was cute.

"My name is Darnel," he said. "I think you are really beautiful. Can I take you out to dinner or a movie?

Not a bad approach. He actually had some manners, despite how young he looked.

We exchanged numbers.

About ten minutes later, I got a text. "It was nice meeting you. Are you still shopping?"

"Yes, I am."

"Did anyone tell you that you have a nice ass?"

I thanked him.

He then sent the most appalling text. "Can you make it clap for me?"

I didn't know how to respond. I was stunned and embarrassed.

"No. I do not get down like that sweetie."

"I figured you wouldn't. You can delete my number."

Only in Walmart.

Tips for the Ladies: Walmart is only for shopping. The tagline is just half right. You can save money but you don't live better.

Tips for the Fellas: Show some respect.

A FLING IS JUST A FLING

I was feeling the Patron, the music was live and I was not ready to leave the party!

The birthday girl and the others in our group left but I stayed behind and got on the dance floor. As I grooved to the music and glanced across the room, my eyes met the eyes of a handsome man that stood about 5'10" with a gorgeous smile and bald head.

We shared a smile. I assumed he wasn't from the area. I could recognize someone from out of town in a heartbeat.

"Why is a sexy woman like you dancing by yourself?" he asked.

"I am quite fine dancing alone and enjoying myself."

"My name is JT. Can I dance with you?"

"Where are you from? Obviously not from around here."

He laughed. "Tennessee. Do I stick out that bad?"

"Yes. Plus the men here don't ask if they can dance with you. They just hop behind you and start dancing."

We danced and talked for about an hour. JT walked me to my car and we talked in the parking lot for another hour. He was in town on business for a month and wanted to see me again. I was feeling his vibe.

As I made my way home, JT called and asked if "again" could be now. I wasn't sleepy so I figured what the hell. He invited me back to his hotel room. We sat and talked a little longer as he began to move in closer. JT was funny, a smooth talker, charming and he smelled so damn good. He was also an Omega man.

He started kissing my neck. I don't usually get down on the first night but I needed a little excitement. I caressed and kissed him back.

He undressed me, touching, kissing and licking all the right places. I

119

drifted into ecstasy.

JT was attentive, gentle and made love to my body like no one had in a very long time. After we climaxed, he held me close as if we'd been together for years.

Later that day, we met for lunch. He said he was in town to make connections for an event his company was launching in cities across the country. Naturally, I was going to help. I invited JT to several events where he met county commissioners, mayors and several business and community leaders. He was appreciative as it made his job a lot easier. But that wasn't all JT was appreciating. We talked several times a day and hung out every night for about two weeks. I was having a blast. The sex was off the chain. Whew!

The fling was great until about the third week. JT had mentioned he was divorced and had two children, the youngest a two-year-old daughter. I was cool with that since I wasn't trying to marry the guy or even be in a relationship for that matter.

JT called to say he wanted to talk. He was feeling me and wanted to make some things firm. I was a bit taken aback because I had no expectations. I was merely having fun. He came to my house later that evening. We sat and joked around for a little bit and then he got serious. He stared into my eyes. "Sugarfoot, I am really digging you. You are smart, beautiful, funny, sexy as hell and ewwww wheeee." Sugarfoot was a nickname JT gave me the first night when I read a flyer on my car and pronounced a performer's name wrong. I just smiled and listened as he talked about being willing to pursue a long-distance relationship.

He asked what I was looking for. I explained that I wasn't seeking a relationship. I was focused on building my business and a few other areas of my life. However, if the opportunity presented itself I was open to a long term relationship that would lead to marriage and a family. I didn't mind a man having children already, however, I wanted children of my own.

JT wasn't sure about having more children, but wanted to give us a try. I asked if he was sure. I was cool with the fun we were having. He assured me that he was serious. I needed a few days to think.

By day three, I told JT I would give the relationship idea a chance. He seemed excited. Over the next few days, JT called less often and I saw him only once that week. The following week was his big event and I didn't hear from or see him at all. As an event planner myself, I tried to be understanding and assumed he was swamped. The week after that, I called and emailed JT and never received a response. In my final email, I told him there were no hard feelings and wished him well.

I told a good friend what happened and he asked if I felt used. I asked in what way. "He needed connections to get his job done," he said, "and it didn't hurt that you were his West Palm Beach girlfriend in the process."

I told my friend I didn't feel used because I had fun and knew exactly what I was getting into.

Tips for the Ladies: Stay focused. If you say you're not interested in a relationship sometimes it's best to stick with that decision even when a man flatters you by claiming he wants something more. There's nothing wrong with a fling. Go for it. You only live once, just have safe fun. Don't feel used if you enjoyed yourself and got something out of the deal.

Tips for the Fellas: Do not feel obligated to give a woman false hope if you are not serious about pursuing a long-term relationship. Many of us can handle a fling and would prefer to leave it at that. It could also be that JT's feelings were hurt because I didn't accept his relationship offer right away. Don't take it personal if a woman needs time and doesn't fall all over you. It's not about you, it's about her.

STOP THE DAMN BICKERING

I am the type of girl who is always up for a challenge but some challenges can be a bit much. Jean Baptiste and I met online. He wanted to meet but each time I made plans with him something came up. The last time was the worst. It was New Year's Eve and Jean wanted to meet before he went to church at eleven. I went shopping with my mom for something to wear later that night. By the time we got home and I got dressed it was after eleven. I figured I'd already missed him and would just call the next day.

I didn't call but a couple days later Jean called me. He thought I was rude to keep him waiting and not call. I agreed. I thought he'd be done with me. Not so much. He still wanted to meet.

We finally did the following week. He came by my office. I was hungry and asked him to take me to a Jamaican restaurant I frequent. Several people struck up conversations with me. Jean sat at the back of the restaurant while I placed my order. He said it was rude of me not to introduce him to anyone and that I acted as if I wasn't with him.

I didn't want to argue so I apologized. I told him that I figured he didn't want to pay for my food since he made no attempt. Jean said he had to go take care of something and dropped me off. I thought that was the end of him.

Not so much.

Jean called every day for about a week. "Ann Marie, when am I going to see you?"

"Well, when would you like to Jean?"

"I'm going to the gym and then I'm going to play racquet ball so I'm not sure."

Why keep calling me every day with the same damn question?
One day, I told Jean I would play racquetball with him if he bought me a racquet. The next day he brought me a racquet. Funny thing is we never played racquetball. After Jean bought the racquet, he started coming by often. He would always ask what I thought of him and how I felt. My response was always the same. "You are cool and I am getting to know you."

I was feisty but he would always say he was going to make me his woman. He was annoying at times but I tolerated him because I had nothing else to do. I liked the attention.

The visits and conversations were consistent for a couple months but I still found Jean annoying because we were always disagreeing about something. We finally went on our first official date. It started rocky.

I told him to surprise me. I wanted him to take control. I had no idea what time he was going to pick me up. About 7:30 p.m. I got a call.
"I am on my way, are you ready?"
"No"
"Why not? You knew we were going out."
I told him I needed about twenty-five minutes. He told me he would be there in ten.
I said whatever and hung up.
I took a shower and was getting dressed when Jean called to say he was outside. I told him I needed another five minutes. He started yelling that he wasn't going to wait. I told Jean to leave and take himself to dinner. He calmed down and said he would wait.

Jean asked where I wanted to go. Didn't he have a plan or reservations? Yes, but I made us late, he said. I wasn't that stupid but at that point I didn't care. I suggested Carrabba's.

He missed the turn then asked me why I didn't tell him. I told him he was driving and would figure it out.

As we parked he complained about the crowd and that the wait would be too long.

It was Friday. There would be a wait anywhere we went.

He fussed about it on the way inside and after the hostess told us it would be twenty-five to thirty minutes, I told him to take me home and proceeded to leave. Jean grabbed my hand, asking why I left him standing there. He'd been complaining all night and I was over the bickering.

We talked in the car, went back in and had dinner. Later that evening Jean rented a hotel room. We discussed taking our acquaintance to another level. The night ended much better than it started.

Jean and I dated for another month. We were always arguing about something. We both had strong opinions and felt we were right. Two events made me realize that being with Jean was not going to work. He called while I was canvassing for a local campaign. I told him where I was and what I was doing but he responded as if he did not understand.

"How can you not understand me?" I asked. "You are the one with an accent."

He yelled that he spoke good English, better than certain blacks I won't name. I hung up before I said something I would surely regret and have folks looking at me crazy.

Jean called me back only to make his point and hang up. I was not about to play that game, so I put him on pause for a couple of days. When I finally decided to answer the phone, I told Jean there were cultural differences that would take some getting used to for both of us. The following week, I was in need of financial assistance. Jean pledged not to help another woman after one he helped a great deal left him.

First, I wasn't that other woman. Second, I wasn't going to be in a relationship with someone not willing to assist me. That was the end.

Tips for the Ladies: Don't get with a man who is constantly bickering about everything you say or do. It just gets crazier from day to day, especially if you, too, are opinionated and headstrong, Not a good combination.

Tips for the Fellas: Leave the bickering to the ladies. Make your point and keep it moving. Don't always be a know-it-all. And do not carry your baggage from a previous relationship into a new one. Don't make the woman in your present pay for the sins of the woman in your past.

FORBIDDEN LOVE AFFAIR

I'd met Basil a few times. He was a friend of my boyfriend Shelton. And his woman was a friend of Shelton. She and I had become pretty cool.

Basil and I hadn't engaged in much conversation during our previous meetings but that changed during a get together at my apartment.

He repeatedly complimented my looks. Didn't I look good the other times he saw me? He told me about his job and short term goals. Then he asked whether I'd be joining Shelton on an upcoming visit. I wasn't invited. Things between Shelton and me were rocky but I didn't let him know. Basil extended an open invitation to stay at his home if I ever visited.

It was awkward because Basil was speaking in front of Shelton and his friends. Of course, Basil's woman wasn't there yet. And he was staring with lust in his eyes. I was attracted to him, too, so I felt uncomfortable. Basil asked that we keep in touch as he was looking for business and employment opportunities in the area.

A month later, Basil called, asking if I was OK. A friend had told him that Shelton and I were breaking up. He heard Shelton was leaving me. Basil said Shelton was a fool. We talked for a couple of hours. It was great having him to talk to. I needed words of encouragement. He also said he was no longer in a relationship.

For the next six months we spoke three to four times per week. We talked about everything from careers to relationships. I felt connected to him. The chemistry was intense. Each time we spoke, he would tell me how I brightened his day. He was happy to hear my voice. By the end of the sixth month, we were talking about seeing each other but were afraid of the consequences.

Our attraction was forbidden. Friendships were on the line.

We were at a crossroads. Do we fall madly in love and forget about our friendships and those we could hurt? Or do we forget about our exes? They had their chance and didn't want us. Should we try being happy together? Was that even realistic considering we lived in different cities and were both vulnerable?

We chose to move on and started seeing other people. We slowed our communication to once a month. We still wanted to see each other and hang out but we were no longer putting brain power into thoughts of what ifs. We agreed that when we saw each other again we would allow nature to take its course.

Five months later, I made a business trip to where Basil lived in New York. I asked if I could crash at his place. He said it was cool. But when I arrived I learned the lady he'd been seeing had moved in and her son was visiting. He asked if I'd be OK staying there. As long as he discussed it with her and they were comfortable, I was cool. It was just a couple of days.

We greeted each other with the biggest hug and he unexpectedly planted the softest kiss on my lips. The feelings that I felt when we talked on the phone came rushing back. Later that evening, we went out to grab a bite and a couple drinks. We talked about our chemistry. Basil said he wished I had come months earlier when he asked again and again. I asked him if it would have made a difference considering he was in a serious relationship now. He said maybe.

We talked about our options. Was it meant for us to just be friends? Should we be intimate and become distant, secret lovers? I didn't have an answer. We had had a few drinks and my hormones and heart started speaking much louder than my mind.

As Basil looked in my eyes, touched my hands, glided his hand across my legs and told me how beautiful I was, I wanted him more and more. I wanted to kiss him. I wanted to feel his warm lips all over me and his soft hands caressing my body. I knew he wanted me. He had the look of sex in his eyes. We left the restaurant and headed back to his house. As we got closer, Basil stopped the car. He reached over and kissed me. It was breathtaking. Heat immediately rushed through my body and between my legs. He kissed my lips and neck and moved slowly to my breasts. His hands caressed my thighs as they moved slowly and gently between them. Then we paused. Basil stopped and stared in my eyes. He told me he had to stop before it got out of control. I assured him that I was not going to let it go any further.

The next day, I watched his woman prepare dinner for more than three hours. She was nice. Basil said he believed she was a good girl. She was smart, clean and could cook. She was the housewife type. He said she wasn't as pretty as me, wasn't business savvy and would not push him like I would but he couldn't get it all in one package. He told me that he loved my drive and ambition and any man would want a woman like me, although I didn't fit in the housewife role. Basil suggested that perhaps he juggle the two of us. I just smiled at him as I thought "Not!" His biggest hesitation, he said, was how we came to know each other. That made it feel wrong for him to love me.

As I watched the way his lady took care of him, I knew he was right. At that time in my life with the pursuit of my goals, I could not give him the time and dedication he needed. I could support his goals and dreams but I just wasn't cut out to be a housewife at that time. Moreover, I felt guilty being in the presence of his lady wanting her man. It was not right eating the food she had prepared and smiling as if I felt nothing for him. I didn't want to be the other woman. I deserved better. I also knew I wouldn't want to be cheated on.

I told Basil he was right and maybe we were just meant to be good friends. I thanked him for helping me through my breakup. I could not have asked for a better friend in that time of need. I wished him much happiness and a successful relationship as we parted ways with hopes that our friendship would stand the test of time.

Things, however, didn't end there. Three years later, I went on a business trip in a city near Basil. He insisted that we have dinner. He took me to a nice resort style restaurant where we dined, talked and laughed for hours. We had a wonderful time. It was apparent we still had strong feelings.

Basil drove me back to my hotel and walked me to my room. We kissed for a while before going inside. He led me to the bed. A part of me knew we were about to cross the line but the rest of me said, "Fuck it. It feels good right now, and I do not want to leave thinking about what if."

The passion exceeded our expectations. It was what we both wanted and needed. Basil held me close until the next morning. We said our goodbyes knowing that no matter what our friendship would prevail.

Tips for the Ladies: Every man is not meant to be your future husband or the person you fall deeply in love with. However, a great friendship can go a long way. If you give into your passion, make sure your friendship will withstand the test of sex, circumstances, and time.

Tips for the Fellas: Be sure the friendship with the woman you comforted and befriended is worth the sacrifice of your friendship with your homeboy and relationship with your current and previous woman.

SIDE CHICK BLUES

Being single is tough, especially when you're focused, busy, and trying to get your life back on track. Dating often takes a back seat. I go through different phases of my singlehood. I take man-cations when I just want to be alone. I get cuddle buddies when I'm too busy. And then there are the times I feel my biological clock ticking and want to settle down.

I was focused on adding some new services to my business and was in my cuddle buddy phase when I met Denzel. We met on Facebook through a mutual friend. Our conversations were always sexually heated. The night we met in person was intense. He was an attractive pecan, medium built, Caribbean. The moment our eyes connected it was on. There was little talking as we had talked enough during the previous weeks. He kissed me with his soft and succulent lips, undressed me while lightly caressing every inch of my body. Shivers went up and down my spine, warm rain showers between my thighs, and my heartbeat raced as if I had been doing high impact Zumba. I was ready to feel every inch of Denzel. My warm, wet punani fit him like a glove. The chemistry was amazing. Our rhythm was in-sync. It was perfect.

For the next ten months, OPP (Other People's Property) and I had a thing going on. I wanted and needed him every weekend, and I mean the entire weekend. When he was unable to come over, I went through Denzel withdrawals. Denzel had a girlfriend who lived seven hours away. He saw her every other month. He had been with her two years when we met. He was honest and upfront about her so I knew what I was getting into. What I did not know or prepare for were the feelings that would develop.

About seven months in, during an intense sexual encounter, Denzel gave me a look I had never seen. "I am bonding with you," he said with a warm smile. "I am feeling feelings for you that I shouldn't be. Why is this happening?"

"Me, too," I said. "I am falling in love with you."

After we had sex and lay in each other's arms, all I could think was "Now, why the hell did I say that? Caught up in the damn moment. What was I thinking?"

From that moment on, crazy thoughts seeped into my mind.

I know the rules of the game. The side chick must stay in her lane; never talk about the main chick and never try to upgrade to be the main chick because it is more than likely not going to happen. So why in the hell was I thinking the opposite?

It didn't help that Denzel started spending more time with me, having deeper conversations and taking me on real dates. My heart wasn't ready for this. I knew it was not going to end well. Somebody was going to get hurt and that somebody would likely be me.

Over the next three months we had a hard decision to make about whether to keep seeing each other. I broke it off but, like an addict, I couldn't stay away too long. I missed his smile, his accent, his soft lips, his touch, the way he felt inside of me, the way we lay in each other's arms, the way he made me smile. He was the ounce of happiness I needed at that time. So we began seeing each other again.

Shortly thereafter, Denzel got a conscience and wanted to come clean about me to his girl because he "now felt like a cheater." Our affair had officially come to an end. It was difficult initially because I really cared about him but I also knew that I was not going to be the chosen one. I was moving into my need to settle down phase and he belonged to another.

Tips for the Ladies: If you knowingly enter a situation as a side chick you have to stick to the side chick rules. Stay in your lane. Never talk about the main chick. Never try to upgrade yourself to be the main chick. Keep your emotions at bay. Know when to exit and just do it. The odds of becoming something other than the side chick are slim to none.

Tips for the Fellas: Do not ever give your side chick any hope that she will become the main chick. Just keep it real and remind her about your circumstance so you both remember it's a relationship of convenience.

FOREVER BACHELOR

I was totally thrown off guard when Robert told me he had been watching me for several years. I knew him from networking events but had never paid him much attention. It wasn't until he introduced me to a friend as the woman who stole his heart that I noticed him. I laughed it off, thinking he was just flirting and went about my business. He found me later and asked if we could get together for dinner over the holidays. "You know where to find me," I said. He never called.

Several months later, we ran into each other and he reminded me that we had not gone out to dinner. I told him to contact me when he was ready. A few weeks later, I lay in bed bored and he ran across my mind so I called him. The call ended with plans for a dinner date the following week.

We met for dinner at a seafood restaurant. He told me how he had a crush on me but didn't know how to approach me. He felt he might be too old for me. He said he wanted a wife and to start a family. He had built his career and accomplished just about everything he had set out to. I was the missing piece of his puzzle.

Robert believed he could make me happy and provide whatever I needed. Since we were in similar professions, he believed we could share ideas and support each other's business.

It sounded pretty good but the brother was pouring it on thick. I told him that I would like to take it slow and see where it goes. He ended the evening by giving me a dozen beautiful pink roses and a kiss on the cheek.

Robert had been enlisted in the armed forces for more than 20 years. He co-owned a newspaper, founded a charity and had a public relations firm. I thought I was busy!

He was retiring from the armed forces in two months and was taking a step back from the charity to just be on the board of directors, which would give him time for a relationship. He had never been married and had no children. He was forty-nine.

I wasn't sure how to feel about his interest given all his endeavors and the fact he had been a bachelor for so long with no children. Was that a red flag?

The following weekend he invited me to dinner. We hung out for a few hours and he seemed really into me. The following weekend, I got concert tickets and invited him to attend. We had planned to meet about six but I noticed the concert had started at eleven thirty that morning so I suggested we grab a movie and dinner. I waited a few hours as he texted me that he was running late. I didn't see him until eleven that evening. I was hotter than fish grease. He sensed it the minute he walked through the door. I asked him right away if this is what I should expect and if so we shouldn't waste time because it wouldn't work for me. He convinced me that it was a unique circumstance. He had three funerals that day, something he didn't think would happen again.

With my schedule and his meetings, military obligations and newspaper deadlines our schedules seemed impossible to sync. He was leaving town for a few days for duty and we agreed to meet the night before his departure. I didn't hear from him until after ten. He stopped by for thirty minutes before saying that he had to leave to meet other obligations. I asked again if this is what I should expect.

"Why are you being so negative?" he asked. "We should focus on the time we have together whether it is five minutes or five hours. Let's just enjoy each other's company." Sounds like something a married man or someone in a relationship would say, I thought.

A couple of weeks passed with the usual brief phone calls and text messages. When I didn't hear from him for a week, I called. He was in Louisiana providing disaster relief to victims of Hurricane Sandy. I understood that duty called. What I couldn't understand is that if I was so important to him, why didn't I know he was leaving and why had I not seen him in weeks?

I told him I understood why he never married. He told me I should show him how to love me the way I wanted to be loved. How was I supposed to teach someone seventeen years my senior how to turn their words into action? How to say "no" to his career and focus on building a relationship and starting a family? Or how to love me?

I just didn't have that kind of time or energy. I didn't feel he was ready to make me a top priority. He talked a good game but didn't back it up. He had a lot of charm and could melt your heart with a bunch of sweet nothings but it was just empty words.

Although he made an effort and helped me with a few things like moving - even then I still didn't have his undivided attention - I was not convinced he was ready to commit to a relationship. Granted I had a busy schedule but people make time for the things that are important to them. I was willing to make time to get to know him.

I kept Robert in the friend zone. He clearly wasn't going to spend the quality time necessary to move our friendship to the next level.

Tips for the Ladies: Action does speak louder than words and old habits are hard to break. When a man says he wants one thing but shows you something different believe what he is showing you. If you meet a man over the age of 45 who has never been married and has no children it's a red flag. He is most likely a "forever bachelor."

Tips for the Fellas: Your actions should match your words. Don't say you are ready to settle down if you're not. Some men aren't meant for serious relationships and plenty of women will date them. Not all women want to be tied down. Be honest about what you want and find a woman who wants the same.

BEEN THERE DONE THAT

At 30, I was at a dating crossroad. Should I date someone my age, younger or older? A younger man might not have the financial security and maturity I was seeking. Guys my age didn't know whether they were ready to settle down. But older men should have it together - financial security, a stable lifestyle, lots of exposure and, of course maturity. Or so I thought.

Steve, "Mr. Been There, Done That," and I attended the same business functions. We went on several dates before I asked what he was looking for. Steve had been married twice, had a 30 year old daughter and a grandson. He was not interested in getting married or having more children. He had been there, done that. He was simply looking for companionship.

Why would he even approach a single woman under thirty-five when she most likely would want to settle down and have babies? He went straight to the friend zone. No emotional attachments, no expectations, no questions about personal affairs. If I chose to have sex it was just to meet my needs.

I was OK with the arrangement because I was going through personal and financial challenges. I needed a friend. Eight months flew by as I tried to work through my personal issues. I was so caught up I didn't even have the time or energy to think about sex.

One night Steve invited me to dinner. We went back to my place to chat and out of nowhere he kissed me passionately. "I have been waiting a long time for this kiss," he said. His hands caressed my face and moved slowly down to my neck and brushed over my breasts, arousing me. My nipples became as hard as chemistry and my panties got wet. He sensed my horniness.

He continued to kiss and caress me while slowly undressing me. His soft tongue made its way slowly down my neck and to my breasts where he gently sucked my nipples. His tongue moved to my navel where he made soft circles. I could hear myself breathing heavily as my heart rate increased. His tongue slowly made its way to the upper section of my pelvis and then slowly down my thighs then back up to the entrance of my lips. He parted them with his hands and used his tongue to search for my clitoris.

I gasped for air and released a soft, passionate moan. He licked and sucked on my clit as if it were the best thing he had tasted in his life. I had never been with someone more than six years older. He was nineteen years my senior and it showed. I could feel the rise of his cock through his pants on my thigh as he came up for air and whispered in my ear. "Do you have a condom?" Regular Trojan or Magnum, I wondered. He had a medium build with small feet and small hands. I chose the Trojan. Right choice.

He gently rubbed his fingers up and down the split of my wet, warm pussy. As he entered me, he whispered, "Damn, this pussy is warm and tight just the way I like it." He moaned and said my name as he moved in and out, repeatedly saying, "Damn this is some good pussy." Just as I was getting my rhythm, he called my name slowly "AMarieeee." His body trembled and I knew it was over. Damn.

I lay still for a while as my pussy throbbed for more but it was over. No round two.
My friend had become my friend with benefits. He knew how to give great head and even work his dick but the dick came too quick.

Over the next year or so, I grew to accept our relationship for what it was. Steve had made his point clear from the beginning. He had been there, done that.

I put up my guard and set my boundaries. To my surprise I was able to keep the mushy emotions out. One day he revealed that he loved me but I wanted to get married. He told me that he would not hold me back from exploring my options and seeking what I wanted. He has been there for me in some of my most difficult times - financially, emotionally and mentally. He never asked questions. It has been a true no strings attached relationship. I appreciate him for his honesty, but more over the friend that he has been outside of the bedroom.

Tips for the Ladies: There are still great men out there who may not be available in the way we want but if we learn to accept that, we can end up with a really great friend and companion. If you learn to separate your emotions it will save you a lot of heartache and may actually bring some joy into your life. You just have to meet people where they are and make sure it is the best situation for you.

Tips for the Fellas: Honesty is the best policy when you are, and we appreciate you so much more. Being considerate of what a woman wants in the long run and allowing her to pursue that is also greatly appreciated.

FRIENDS TIL THE END

Freshman year at FAMU, my sister Elaine and I went to a Kappa party at the Ming Tree restaurant. We were dancing our asses off when this big black dude came up to me and said, "Goddamn, where are you from, dancing like that? You are really shaking your ass!" I rolled my eyes and kept dancing. "You are cute too," he said. "What's yo name?" I said, "Ann," and kept on dancing. He smiled and walked off saying he would be back.

After the party, my sister and I were walking to the car when the big black dude showed up again, "Ann, where are you going when you leave here?"
"Home."
"Wait up. Let me holla at you for a second."
I was not that interested. He wasn't that cute and looked like a football jock. I was not into dating football players. Still, I stopped to see what he had to say.

Ronald had my sister and me rolling with laughter in the parking lot for several minutes before he asked if he could call me. He was funny as hell so I said, "Yes," but told him I had a boyfriend.

Ronald called me every day for the next couple of weeks, always asking to hang out after football practice. "We can go to the bowling alley. Let's just walk around campus. Come over to the boys' dorm." Really? I turned him down. I had a boyfriend whom I liked. We were really into each other.

Soon after, I had a horrible week. I had just come back from home because my mom had been in the hospital. I got fired from my job for going home to see my mom. I had C's in all of my classes and I was already on academic probation. To top it all off, my boyfriend had enlisted in the Marines and didn't tell me until two days before that he was leaving.

I was overwhelmed. Ronald called me at the right time and asked me to come and walk around campus with him. I told him everything that was going on and he was very attentive. He gave me good advice. We talked for hours. He was much more intelligent than I thought and he kept me laughing. I was happy we had become friends. Ronald and I talked every day for the rest of the semester. I would ask him when he was taking me out to dinner or the movies and he would say some silly shit like, "Man, I'm a broke college student. We can have dinner in the cafeteria. You order whatever you want to eat, get seconds and free refills. I will bring some candles to make it romantic." Or, "We can go to the movies on Thursday. It's free movie night in Lee Hall every Thursday. Just put some popcorn in your purse."

Right before summer break, Ronald asked if I was staying for the summer. I was. I needed to take classes to bring my GPA up so I would not flunk out. He insisted that I be his lady. I agreed since he had been there for me and we had learned so much about each other.

Ronald and I dated for about a month before football practice picked up for the fall. At first, we continued to talk every day but we only saw each other a few times because we both had jobs; I was now working at Cash America Pawn. I had moved off campus a good distance from him and had summer classes. Ronald got busy with practice, so I only heard from him a few times a week either early in the morning or late at night. I got upset and told him he needed to make time for me. He said he was trying but it was tough with two-a-day practices, study hall and the rest of his obligations. He said it would get better in the spring. I was not trying to hear that, so I told him to call me in the spring and hung up.

Ronald and I didn't talk much for the next several months, but no matter where he saw me, he would stop and speak even if it meant blocking traffic. By the end of senior year, we had remained good friends and helped each other out of crazy situations. I moved to South Florida after graduation. I didn't tell Ronald goodbye or get his contact information, so I didn't think I would see him again.

The following year, I went to homecoming and met up with some of my friends. We went out and when the night was over I heard someone say, "Ann, you just gonna walk past like you don't know me?" It was Ronald. I walked over and gave him a big hug. We talked for a few minutes and exchanged numbers. I was happy to see him. Familiar emotions came rushing back.

Since then, Ronald and I have never lost touch. He has become one of my best friends in the world. We have shared war stories about our loves and losses. We have watched and supported each other grow personally and professionally. He adores the woman I have grown into and I am so proud of the man he has become.

Over the years, we've discussed the possibilities of a romantic relationship but something always came up. Ex-girlfriend called and said she was pregnant. He got shot. I got a live-in boyfriend. He moved in with a woman. We figure we are just meant to be good friends.

I did tell him that if I do not get married and have a baby by 36, he would have to be my sperm donor. He happily agreed to be my future baby daddy if necessary. Ronald and I cannot go more than three months without speaking. We absolutely love each other.

When I need a laugh, to talk to a familiar voice - a real deal Holyfield who is going to tell me when I'm wrong, someone who will always encourage me to do better, someone I can borrow a few dollars from that I probably won't pay back, or someone who will just brighten my day, I call on Ronald. He is my friend 'til the end...or so I thought. The truth is I held on to a belief and delusional hope that maybe one day Ronald would be the love of my life, my knight and shining armor, my friend and lover to the end. Deep down inside, I believed that he would see me for the wonderful person I am, stop searching for love and ask me to be his wife to grow old with. I would be the one to give birth to his first daughter. One day, a harsh reality set in and I had to let go and move on from an empty past.

On not one, but two occasions, I made travel plans and arrangements to see Ronald and in both instances, he left me hanging out to dry. The first occasion, I had to cancel my flight and use the airline ticket for another destination because he had a new girlfriend. Second and final instance, he also had a new girlfriend, however told me that he had an open door for me. Days before my arrival, I reminded him of my upcoming trip to New Orleans and asked him to pick me up from the airport, he simply stated he didn't think that was going to happen because he had a lot going on - he knew about my trip months prior. Upon my arrival, I called to let him know how long I would be in town and where I was staying, since my original plans of staying at his mom's or his place fell through. He insisted that he would not allow me to come to town and not come by and spend time with me. For the next seven days that I was in New Orleans, I did not receive as much as a text message to ask if I was okay or safe. As I took time to reflect, the truth hit me that all these years, I was the one doing most of the calling, texting, planning, and loving. I kept the "friendship" going.

I knew as I prepared to leave New Orleans and return to Florida, that I had to leave him and what I thought was a true friendship behind. I had to let go of my self-inflicted delusions that there could be more. Ronald had moved on a long time ago, but I was stuck in what could have and should have been.

Tips for the Ladies: Never judge a book by its cover. You never know who that person may turn out to be in the long run. Keep an open mind. Every relationship you have with a man doesn't have to be romantic. Sometimes timing, distance or just life prevents that. Appreciate the love and laughter of a platonic relationship. If it ends up being romantic, too, great! Enjoy it! Moreover, know when to let go. If you are doing all the pursuing, maybe you have created a delusion that it is more than it really is. Truth of the matter is if he is not pursuing you and the friendship as much as you are, it is just an illusion to move on from.

Tips for the Fellas: Keep a smile on her face, joy in her soul, and positive words of encouragement in her time of need and you will earn a friend for life who will always be there. However, if and when you believe that season of friendship has ended, let her know so she can move on.

CONCLUSION

I am a serial dater, but I hate dating. It seems like a necessary evil that is fun and intriguing while time consuming and exhausting. I have dated guys that are nice, educated, professional, wealthy, poor, intelligent, indecisive, insecure, unavailable, busy, preoccupied, divorced, separated, an emotional wreck, fine as hell, a few extra pounds, short, tall, rugged, metro and more. I have met them all. Yet, I am not with any of them today. Have I been an angel through this journey? Admittedly, I have not. I am smart, sexy, beautiful, loving, kind, supportive, humorous, but at times self-centered, rude, selfish, naive, heartless, and an emotional roller coaster.

Dating has brought me joy, happiness, love, and compassion. However, it has brought me much frustration, pain, disappointment, and emptiness. The constant search for a compatible companion is tiring. There are times where I want to give up because true love seems so farfetched. I think about and sometimes act on my emotion of being a cold, heartless bitch, but my heart tells me there is hope and I should hold on because God is going to send me the right person in due time.

Over my 20 years of dating, the process and landscape has changed. It is complicated. Today, most do not want to work for a relationship, have a desire for courtship, or want to take time to get to know someone. It is all about instant gratification. I am guilty of it. There were times where a quick fling was just enough based on the phase of my life or the fact that I was horny and needed some action. However, what I always wanted was romance, love, and my forever man. He has not arrived (or he has not arrived again). So the saga continues.

I may meet someone nice that I am not attracted to, patient with, or just do not understand. He may be the one, but I may not realize it until he is gone. I may meet someone that is not ready, too busy, has baggage, and wants a side chick or mistress, or a place holder. I am confident that there will be a time that I will meet someone that will complement me and me him. I will not have to wonder or guess if he is the one, I will just know. I will feel it in every part of my body and spirit. The connection will be real and we will both recognize it. I will not have to compromise who I am or what I want. He will stand by me through the test of time. He will be my life partner until death do us part.

In the meantime, I will embrace and date by the twelve serial dater affirmations that I discovered through my journey.

1. Fear... Face Everything and Rise
2. I am priority #1
3. I am a big fucking deal
4. Say It Early
5. I am Doing Me
6. Trust my gut
7. Change no one
8. Look in the Mirror
9. I've Got the Power
10. On to the Next One
11. Date and Keep the Faith
12. Be honest, be real, be me

SERIAL DATER AFFIRMATIONS

Fear... Face Everything and Rise

Fear... face everything and rise. Fear has been my motivator and inhibitor. Fear of the unknown, commitment, what others will think, or that this just might work out has contributed to how successful my relationships have been. I choose to be motivated by fear and face every positive possibility head on and desire a partner who will do the same.

I am Priority #1

I have always put others first over myself. In relationships, it has been no different as I have placed my feelings, wants, needs, expectations, sexual desires and pleasures on the back burner. It took a few situations for me to realize that I had to make myself the number one priority before I could expect someone else making me theirs. I am selfish and I put me first.

I am a Big Fucking Deal

I am a big fucking deal! I have been told that I am intimidating, strong, aggressive, demanding, overpowering, too smart, too confident, and much more, all of which have made me question if I should somehow tone it all down so "he" will date me. Why should I shrink myself or dim my light to make someone else feel secure? Get over it! I know my value and worth and "he" that cannot accept it, kick rocks!

Say it Early

What do I want, expect, am willing to accept and willing to give? Save time and lay it all out on the table in the beginning. I must be clear about what I want and communicate it from day one. I must be purposeful, direct, and not hide behind what "he" is going to think if

I show my cards too soon. Time is the one thing I cannot get back, so why waste it.

I am Doing Me

I am doing me! I play by my rules and on my terms. I will date who, what, when, and how I want. I set my standards and decide when they are to be compromised. I can be conservative or promiscuous. It is my life and I will live it as I see pleasing to me and my God.

Trust My Gut

My instincts are razor sharp. I know when something is going great and when something is going terribly wrong, but have at times made the decision to ignore that nagging feeling in my gut (often bad decision). I will trust my instincts because 99 percent of the time, they are correct.

Change No One

I have believed that I could change a person's mind, feelings, situation, action, or something about them I didn't like. I was so wrong, people don't change unless they want to and we can't change anyone but ourselves.

Look in the Mirror

I must take a regular self-assessment to evaluate my behaviors, patterns, happiness, and my role in the relationship (or situationship). A few questions I must ask myself are: Can I make improvements? Can I bring more to the situation? Is this a happy and healthy place for me? Should I take a step back or away from the person?

I've Got the Power

I have the power within me to create my destiny, but I cannot control someone else's actions or make them marry me (I wish I had that kind of power). I have the power to make someone treat me the way I want and deserve to be treated, allow positivity into my space, and to walk away if it is not making me happy.

On to the Next One

I refuse to be unhappy, stressed, or surrounded by drama! I will not get comfortable or be afraid to let go when I am hurting physically, emotionally, mentally, and spiritually. I will not be afraid to be alone. Moreover, I will move on to the next one. Life is short, so I will enjoy it with someone who wants to enjoy it with me.

Date and Keep the Faith

There is someone for everyone (I have seen some unbelievable couples). I have faith that my future husband is waiting for our paths to cross (or cross again). In the meantime, I will date the right person for this season.

Be Honest, Be Real, Be Me

I will always be honest with myself and who I date. I will always be real and bring my authentic self. I am my greatest discovery.

ABOUT ANN MARIE SORRELL

Ann Marie Sorrell is a philanthropist, full-figured model, award-winning business leader, woman of faith and emboldened enthusiast of the opposite sex. She lives out loud and is unapologetic in her support of the many causes that are important to her, which include: social justice, equality for all, issues impacting women and minorities, economic development and health & wellness. She is the President & CEO of The Mosaic Group (mosaicgroup.co), and Founder of MustAttend Events, Inc (mustattend.co). Ann Marie earned a Master of Business Administration from Nova Southeastern University and Bachelor of Science in Health Care Management from Florida A&M University. Ann Marie serves on several community boards and has won numerous awards for her leadership, business acumen, and community involvement.

The quest for love is very challenging for a busy professional, but it has not stopped Ann Marie in her pursuit to meeting and settling down with Mr. Right. Her journey through the good, bad, funny - and steamy - of dating and relationships inspired her to document the twists and turns as she believed certainly she could not be the only one experiencing these types situations. The writings lead to Chronicles of a Serial Dater.

In her spare time, she enjoys, music, dancing, golf, traveling, meeting new people and flirting. She currently resides in West Palm Beach, Florida.